Joel Gerschman is a leading coach, author and educator in the field of business growth, management and leadership. Drawing on more than 15 years of battle-tested experience running multiple fast-growing technology start-ups and learning under some of the world's leading business gurus, including Michael Gerber, author of *The E-Myth Revisited*, Joel has helped thousands of business leaders to achieve more stability, more financial freedom and more time … for life. Joel also brings a unique perspective to managing the people-side of business growth. With his background as a commercial lawyer and years of experience as mediator and university lecturer in negotiation, conflict resolution and influential communication, Joel is an expert in the psychology of influencing human behaviour. He is the founder and CEO of a leading business coaching company called The Change Coach (thechangecoach.co), as well as a co-creator of *The Mindful Entrepreneur's* Growth System — a proven, step-by-step system to grow your revenue, your free time and your sense of fulfilment (www.mindfulentrepreneur.co). Joel lives in Melbourne, Australia with his wife and four children.

Howard Finger is a serial entrepreneur, and a builder and leader of online collaborative communities. Howard has nurtured start-ups from ideas to hyper-growth and market dominance, and has transitioned established analogue businesses into online marketplaces,.

culminating in IPOs valued at hundreds of millions of dollars. Howard is CEO and founder of VinciWorks, the leading provider of GRC training, software and services to the world's largest law firms and other top professional firms. VinciWorks' driving purpose is to create a safer, fairer and more honest world (vinciworks.com). Previously, Howard was a partner at a leading Hong Kong law firm, and Senior VP at Global Sources, the NASDAQ-listed facilitator of global merchandise trade. Howard lives in Melbourne, Australia with his wife and two daughters. He holds a black belt in karate and is a published author. As co-creator of *The Mindful Entrepreneur's* Growth System, Howard strives to live his purpose every day: to create the greatest sustainable value – no excuses!

Rabbi Aryeh Goldman has dedicated his life to helping his students and clients actualise their potential. As an ordained Rabbi, qualified teacher and counsellor for over 20 years, Aryeh blends the ancient wisdom of his heritage with the most cutting-edge and effective mindfulness techniques to provide a truly holistic approach to personal fulfilment and wellbeing. Aryeh writes a regular blog on mindful, intentional and meaningful living through a Jewish lens (amindfuljew.com) and is a co-creator of *The Mindful Entrepreneur's* Growth System (www.mindfulentrepreneur.co). Aryeh lives in Melbourne, Australia with his wife and six children.

The *Mindful* Entrepreneur

Joel Gerschman
Howard Finger and Aryeh Goldman

XOUM PUBLISHING

Sydney

XOUM

First published by Xoum in 2017

Xoum Publishing
PO Box Q324, QVB Post Office,
NSW 1230, Australia
www.xoum.com.au

ISBN 978-1-925143-45-4 (print)
ISBN 978-1-925143-46-1 (digital)

Cataloguing-in-publication data is available from the National Library of Australia

Cover design by Xou Creative, www.xoucreative.com.au
Printed and bound in Australia by McPherson's Printing Group

Papers used by Xoum Publishing are natural, recyclable products made from wood grown in sustainable forests. The manufacturing processes conform to the environmental regulations of the country of origin.

To our wives and children, who light up our lives
and give us the drive to pursue our purpose

CONTENTS

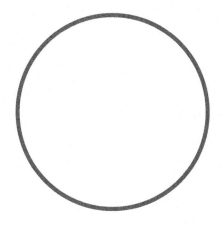

INTRODUCTION

Is it possible to turn around your business – and your life – in a single year? Maybe in legends and fairytales, right? Classic books and movies are full of fictional heroes who step up to a challenge, battle adversity and come out on top. But does it happen in real life? And is there *anything* that ordinary, mere mortals like you and I can learn from these stories?

Howard Finger's personal and business transformation *is* based on real life. Most of it also happened within a year. But let me back up a minute to give you some context. There are three key characters in this story: Howard Finger, the embattled but gritty small business owner, he is the protagonist; Aryeh Goldman, Howard's guru and mentor on mindful living; and me, the business coach who helps Howard to save and then grow his business. I don't want to spoil the story so I'll leave the details about how we came to mentor Howard until later. But I do want to tell you *why* we wrote this book.

After working with Howard for some months, we began to see incredible results. He veered away from a fast-approaching business collapse and intensely stressful life towards a profitable, growing business and a deeper sense of personal wellbeing and fulfilment. We decided to chronicle his experiences because the transformational process that Howard undertook is entirely replicable, and could therefore help other business owners like you.

But make no mistake. This isn't simply another business book. Nor is it another self-help manual on mindfulness. Instead, it's a *holistic* approach to surviving and thriving in business that fuses proven, cutting-edge business strategy with powerful psychological practices.

The state of your business and your state of mind are deeply intertwined. A chaotic, cash-strapped business that consumes all of your time will profoundly impact your stress levels and your sense of satisfaction. Likewise, your ability to cope with stress and maintain internal balance will significantly affect your capacity to run a successful business. Dealing with only one of these dimensions will leave the other wanting. It takes a holistic approach to deliver the outcomes that business owners truly desire: a successful business *and* a real sense of personal fulfilment.

To help you achieve these outcomes, *The Mindful Entrepreneur* offers a practical, holistic approach that focuses on three key areas:

1. Generating **rapid, profitable growth** to fund your desired lifestyle;

2. Making your business run **without your constant involvement**, so you have the space, time and freedom to focus on *each* area of your life, not just work; and

3. Building your **capacity** to stay sane, focused and fulfilled while managing the inevitable challenges, stressors and disappointments that life throws at you.

There's another reason why this isn't your run-of-the-mill business or self-help book: it straddles two vastly different styles. Think of it as 'gripping non-fiction novel meets intensive training seminar'. What do I mean? Firstly, it's a true story written *as a story*, not as a typical 'how-to' manual. It's a real-life, warts-and-all account of how Howard saved and grew his business, written in a relaxed, 'conversational' tone with only minor chronology and contextual changes to ensure a coherent narrative. Secondly, the book is more than just an interesting story; it's also a highly practical *guide*, filled with strategies, examples and tools that you can apply immediately. At the end of each chapter you'll find concise summaries, combined with links to downloadable resources, to aid your application.

Finally, while the holistic approach and the book's style are unique, its core principles are not. They're inspired by some of the most effective strategies developed by leading authorities across the business, psychology and spiritual fields. *The Mindful Entrepreneur* draws heavily, for example, on the work of my own mentor, Michael

Gerber, author of the business classic, *The E-Myth Revisited*, and often referred to as the world's number one small business guru. Jim Collins, author of *Good to Great*, Simon Sinek, author of *Start with Why*, and the ground-breaking works of psychiatrists such as Aron Beck and Victor Frankl also find expression in the pages that follow, along with the works of many others. *The Mindful Entrepreneur* is as much a paean to them and their pioneering work as it is a vivid demonstration of how their ideas changed Howard's business and life.

We hope you enjoy *The Mindful Entrepreneur* and that you learn practical strategies and tools to rapidly grow your own business while staying sane, focused and fulfilled.

Joel Gerschman

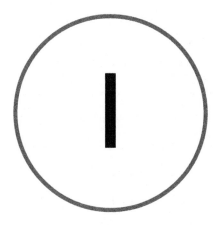

A DIFFICULT TIME

Howard woke. It was dark outside. He looked at the clock: 3 a.m. With a groan, he closed his eyes. As he lay there, his mind churned with worry and confusion. His e-learning business was in trouble. The overdraft was almost at its limit, his credit cards were maxxed out, and there was no cash. He couldn't sell either of his cars because the out-standing lease payments exceeded their values. In that dark hour before dawn, he played out all the dismal scenarios that accompany business failure. He knew that even if he could come up with some miracle solution it would likely take too long to implement in time to generate enough revenue to pay the most critical bills. He knew that he was on his own. No one was going to come to his rescue. The future of his business was entirely up to him.

He owed his subcontracted development and support team £80,000 – or six months' money. They hadn't told him how bad their own cash-flow problems were and that they hadn't even been paying their own Value Added Tax (VAT) bills. Now the UK VAT Office was going to lock their doors if they didn't pay the whole amount by the end of the month. If the subcontractor stopped work, there would be no technical support for Howard's existing clients, he wouldn't be able to set up new clients, the new products in development would never get finished, and the entire business – the baby that Howard had carefully nurtured for five years – would implode.

It wasn't just his company that was in trouble. His professional life and his personal life were inextricably linked like two trees whose roots intertwine deep underground. Howard lived in Australia but most of his business revenue was generated in the UK. The exchange rates were killing him, and hence the school fees for both of his children were overdue. As he lay in the dark, he struggled to figure out what he would say to his kids when he needed to pull them out of the schools they loved.

He looked at his wife, Andrea, sleeping next to him. That evening she'd told him of her embarrassment when their credit cards had been rejected at the local grocery store. She was such a strong and forgiving woman, and it broke Howard's heart that he had let her down. It was harder for her because she had no control over their situation. Howard felt that he couldn't further burden her with his fears and concerns.

This was not what he'd anticipated when he started his own business. He'd hoped it would give him financial freedom, more time and more control over his destiny. Instead, he felt like a slave. The business was consuming his life rather than serving it. It wasn't meant to be this way. He thought about their life insurance policy. If he were gone there would be enough money to sustain Andrea and the kids for several years. It would be a gift. *No! Don't even think about it!* he remonstrated. No matter how bad his life might be, it would be a cowardly and grievous mistake to even consider death as a solution. He rolled over, desperate to go back to sleep just so he could stop thinking and worrying. He even began whispering to G-d, begging for the miracle of divine intervention.

The alarm went off at 6.30 a.m. and Howard realised he had fallen back to sleep. But that ugly, sick feeling in the pit of his stomach told him that despite being in his comfortable bed, he was neither rested nor refreshed. He also knew that hiding under the covers was not the answer.

Andrea woke up, opened her eyes and smiled bravely at him.

Howard threw off the blanket, put his feet on the floor, rubbed his eyes and resolved to meet the challenges of the new day. He knew it was up to him to find the answers. He was also wise enough to realise that he needed help. Who could give him sound, non-judgmental advice?

At breakfast, he put on a cheerful face for the kids. Andrea knew something was bothering him, but she also knew that when the time was right, he'd open up to her.

As he was driving to the office, Howard decided to contact his co-shareholders, two old friends who lived in Hong Kong. When he had started the company, they'd helped with some working capital in return for a small percentage in the business. It was embarrassing, but Howard recognised he had no choice but to go back and ask them if they would lend the business more money to keep it alive.

Once at his desk, he sorted through the emails that had piled up since he had left the office a scant ten hours earlier. There were several customer service issues and a request for a quotation from the sales manager. The content manager wanted approval for an update to one of the online courses. The accountant wanted copies of last year's bank statements and an explanation on expenses. There were four emails from the subcontractor desperate for money to pay his VAT and a third request from the landlord for last month's office rent. Howard hadn't even bothered to listen to the voice messages from the bank about the overdraft.

He sighed. It would take him at least an hour to reply to the emails, and he would have to speak to the bank and then deal with more emails from employees, clients and suppliers with other questions and more problems.

Ignoring the messages, Howard booked a meeting with his co-shareholders before using the rest of the overdraft to buy an economy flight ticket to Hong Kong. He felt relief at having decided to seek their advice. Simply admitting to himself that he had a problem, and taking the first step to solving it, made him feel a little more positive about his future.

There was a knock on the door.

'Come in,' said Howard as he clicked off the airline website. He looked up to see his friend, Joel Gerschman.

'Hi, Howard, is this a good time?' Joel asked. 'You told me to pop by to discuss the extra desk in your office. Is it still available?'

'Yes,' replied Howard with a forced smile. He didn't want Joel to notice his anxiety. 'Come on in. There's the spare desk — please make yourself at home. I'm happy to share my space.'

Joel put his laptop bag and keys down. 'I really appreciate this.'

'No problem. It seems like a fair deal — you need some office space and I could do with some help with the rent.'

'Actually, I'd like more than just a desk.'

'Oh really?' Howard cringed inside, hoping that Joel was not going to ask for a loan. 'What else do you want?'

'I want some of your time and your expertise,' Joel said as he sat down. 'I want some help to determine if and how I could leverage online technology to scale my business coaching practice.'

Howard clicked off the message he was reading and leaned back in his chair. 'Joel, I'm happy to help, but I don't know anything about your coaching business.'

'I can explain it to you. It's not brain surgery!'

Howard rubbed his eyes and considered his own predicament. He wondered if Joel's coaching program might allow him to take a fresh look at his own business and help him in some way. What harm was there in trying? And perhaps some sort of exchange would make Joel happy.

'I'll tell you what,' Howard said. 'The way things are right now, I might get something out of your business coaching. Why don't we do a barter exchange? I'll give you the desk and you put me through your coaching program. I assume I'll get some value from it, and then I might be better positioned to advise you on how to leverage online learning to scale your business.'

'I'd be delighted to do that,' replied Joel. 'When would you like to begin?'

Howard looked at his inbox. Like the steady drip from a tap that could never be fixed, the messages were not going to stop. There would never be a good time to begin. With a sudden surge of decisiveness, he looked Joel in the eye and said, 'How about right now? I have an hour to spare.'

'Really?'

'I'm leaving for Hong Kong tomorrow, and it'd be good to have begun before I go away. There's no time like the present, right?'

'Okay,' said Joel. He swung his chair around to face Howard and folded his hands in his lap. 'Please begin by telling me a bit about your business, including why you started it.'

GOOD ADVICE

Howard had been working for Global Sources, a large trade magazine publishing company, and was responsible for transitioning the business from print to online. Over the years he accrued a wellspring of experience, generating over $40 million dollars a year in online subscription-based revenues and working with over 500 salespeople across 20 countries.

To achieve his goal of converting a large multinational sales team of Yellow Pages-type advertising salespeople into online internet 'solutions providers', Howard had developed a basic form of online learning. It was really just PowerPoint via email, but he was impressed with the effectiveness and speed with which he'd managed to educate a large group of geographically dispersed individuals. That's when he first got hooked on the idea of online learning.

Then the dot-com world imploded and, virtually overnight, Howard went from being seemingly indispensable to instantly disposable. He was made redundant. Although it sounds trite, redundancy is one of those deeply painful events that can change a person's life. Indeed, while the sense of rejection and worthlessness can be immense, redundancy can also create opportunities one might not otherwise have seen or acted upon.

Howard took advantage of the moment of personal reflection that had been forced upon him. Rather than immediately moving into another corporate role, he decided to change direction. He decided to go out on his own and create his own e-learning business. The idea seemed feasible; in the industry he was considered an internet and e-learning guru.

'You know the phrase,' said Howard as Joel listened, '*In the land of the blind the one-eyed man is king*. Well, that was me. I had already used e-learning to help Global Sources launch a successful B2B website and community, so why couldn't I do it for myself? That way, I could control my destiny, never again endure the sting of redundancy, make my own decisions, choose when I wanted to work, earn more money and possibly use e-learning to make an impact on the world.' He smiled wryly. 'At least that was the dream.'

'And have you been able to achieve those goals – at least to some degree?' asked Joel.

'If I'm honest, I'd probably say no. I started VinciWorks five years ago and although I've built a business with an impressive customer base made up of most of the world's top law firms, I'm under constant financial pressure. Cash flow is always tight and there's never enough money to allow me to live the lifestyle I'd hoped for. I'm always stressed, fighting fires and feeling like everything depends on me because I can't rely on others to do the job right. I wish I had more time for those really important things I never seem to get around to doing – things like spending time with my family and friends, playing golf, or just creating time and space to breathe. Rather than having a business that serves me, I feel like I'm a slave to my business.'

'Look, this might not make you feel any better, but many business owners face a similar reality,' said Joel. 'Their businesses consume rather than serve them. It's a widespread problem.'

'Yes, I know I'm not the first guy to face a tough battle,' said Howard. 'But it certainly feels like everyone is successful except me.'

'Well, it's possible to change that reality,' said Joel. 'I've helped numerous business owners do it.'

'I'd like to believe you, but I'll need to be convinced.'

'You always were stubborn!' said Joel with a laugh. 'But that's good. Your tenacity will prevent you from giving up. But let's not get ahead of ourselves; the proof will be in the results.'

IDENTIFY THE PROBLEM

Joel leaned forward. 'The first step is to understand what's causing your current challenges. By this I don't mean the *symptoms*, I mean the *root causes*. For example, if your company has poor sales, that's not a cause of your problems, it's a symptom of something fundamental that's not working. Therefore, simply saying, "We're going to increase our sales" is misguided; it does no good to attack only the symptom. Once we understand the root causes we can begin working on solutions. You mentioned that cash flow is tight, for example. What do you think is causing that issue?'

'I'll try to retrace the problem back to its source,' said Howard. 'I believe that we have cash-flow issues because we have too many customers who don't pay on time. On top of that, our salespeople aren't hitting their sales targets. And, to be honest, our customers – the legal sector in particular – still haven't fully recovered from the global financial crisis.'

Joel smiled. 'I don't doubt that any of those are contributing factors. But it's interesting to note that everything you mentioned lies *outside* of you. It's your salespeople, or your customers, or the financial crisis. Do you think it's possible that you, as the CEO, have a part to play, too?'

Howard felt his neck muscles tighten. This was not what he expected. He was looking for sympathy and for someone to commiserate with him. Joel's question sounded like one that would come from his father or a schoolteacher.

'What are you saying – that it's my fault?' he said.

Joel raised his hands, palms showing. 'No, of course not. It's rarely that simple. The factors you mentioned are real and relevant. What I want you to see is that both the mindset and the skillset of the owner – the individual who has the power and authority to lead the business – play a crucial role. And that's not intended as an insult. It's actually empowering. With the right mindset and the right skillset, you can shape your own reality – at least to a larger extent than you seem to be doing right now.'

'In some circles I'm considered the "father of online learning",' said Howard, 'and I've been doing it for more than a decade. How can you say I don't have the right mindset or the right skillset?'

Joel smiled again. 'Your online learning expertise is unsurpassed. That's a given. It's why I came to you in the first place. My point is that most new businesses are formed by people just like you. The owners are genuinely skilled and experienced in a certain technical field. Then they decide they'd rather work for themselves than for someone else. Their new business takes off with lots of energy, just like yours; yet despite their skills and experience, they struggle to make their businesses work.'

'Why?'

'Many of them make a dangerous assumption: that because they're good at *doing the work* of their business, they can create a business *that works*. Unfortunately, it's untrue. It's a fantasy. In his book, *The E-Myth Revisited*, business guru Michael Gerber calls it the "entrepreneurial myth" – and it's the central reason most businesses fail to thrive.'

Howard fiddled with a pencil. Joel's words were beginning to resonate. 'I suppose you're right. To go from minding your own little corner of the store to being in charge of every department is not as easy as it seems.'

'Exactly. I bet that shortly after starting your business, you realised that there were many areas with which you were unfamiliar – such as creating a marketing strategy; raising funds; bookkeeping; collections; and managing staff, both onsite and remote. Is that right?'

'I suppose that's right.'

'What did you do about all that "unfamiliar" work?'

'I figured it out by trial and error,' said Howard. 'I learned how to do some of it by my own effort. But the truth is, I probably just ignored certain things because I wasn't sure what to do – like marketing strategy and financial management. I struggle to get my head around the financial side – bookkeeping, accounting, spread-sheets, taxes, depreciation and all of that. So I focused on what I knew I was good at – the hands-on work of designing, developing, and selling our core e-learning services to customers.'

'Many entrepreneurs do exactly that.'

'But is that really a bad thing?' said Howard. 'The business grew on the back of my passion, energy, experience and skill in doing that work.'

'Right,' said Joel. 'And you should be applauded for your effort.

It's no mean feat. But now you've reached a plateau. Otherwise you wouldn't be talking to me.'

'The edge of a cliff is a more accurate description,' said Howard with a sigh. 'I'm so busy and stressed just doing what you call the "technical" work that I have neither the time nor the headspace to even begin thinking about growth. There are always fires to put out, complaints to deal with, urgent administrative work to do, bills to pay – it goes on and on. I'm consistently focused on survival. And truth be told, even if I found the time, I'm not entirely sure I'd know how to grow the business. What's worse, I'm not even happy doing what I'm doing any more. There are moments I enjoy but I do wonder what it's all for.'

'It's nothing to be ashamed of,' said Joel. 'As I said, it's common. But if you want to move your business and your life forward, you'll need a fundamentally different mindset and skillset. You can't just be a great technician; you need to be a great manager and a great entrepreneur, too.'

BALANCE THREE ROLES

Joel explained that to be successful, you must effectively balance three distinct roles.

'At times you need to be what Michael Gerber calls a *technician*, doing the operational work of the business that delivers value to customers.

'You also need to be a *manager* who is overseeing, planning, organising and supervising others to ensure they get the work done effectively.

'And perhaps most critically, you need to be an *entrepreneur*, doing the strategic work of building the business itself by clarifying your vision, innovating improved ways of doing things and identifying new markets and opportunities.

'The problem is that most business owners are so focused on the day-to-day technical work that they never even begin thinking about how to better manage or build their business. That's the "technician" mindset at work.

'Technicians spend their time working in their business, hoping that things will eventually change and they won't have to work so hard for so little in return. But the reality is that things won't change. Not until you change the way your business runs. And that requires working *on* your business, not just *in* your business. Michael Gerber coined that phrase by the way,' noted Joel.

'You seem to quote him a lot.'

'Yes, in many ways his ideas revolutionised the field of small business management,' said Joel. 'I learned a great deal of what I know from him. It's only fair to acknowledge my sources.'

'Well, I've heard that idea of working *on* my business before,' said Howard, 'but no one ever explains how to do it or is willing or able to provide the support to implement it. I've been to conferences and listened to great speakers saying similar stuff. But then the fires explode, I get distracted and nothing changes.'

'That's what my business is all about,' said Joel. 'I break it down into small digestible components that can be implemented one piece at a time, and then I support you through the process. There are thousands of business owners like you who struggle with this process because it requires you to view your business from a fundamentally different perspective.

'Working on your business requires you to step outside of your day-to-day technical work,' continued Joel. 'It means looking at your business objectively, as if it were something independent of you. Imagine you're 5000 feet above your business, looking down on it, critically. Only from that perspective can you truly begin designing your business to operate as smoothly, efficiently and profitably as possible. Of course, this demands real objectivity on your part – which isn't easy to achieve alone.'

'Okay. It makes sense in theory. But where do I start?'

BREAK FREE

'It all depends on your goals,' said Joel. 'If all you care about is revenue growth, for example, I'd focus on your marketing and sales strategy. In your case, though, my sense is that your aim isn't just growth; it's also about setting up your business to run smoothly and profitably without your constant involvement. You want to be able to avoid the everyday stress and get back to your family. Is that right?'

'Yes, that's exactly what I'm after.'

'In that case you'll need to start by doing something quite radical: you'll have to break free of your business.'

'What?' asked Howard, a little confused.

Joel stood up and went to the window. He pulled open the shade so that natural light flooded the room. Then he turned to Howard. 'Do you find yourself saying, "If I'm not doing the work, watching it, making it happen, then it just doesn't happen – at least not properly?"'

'Yes, all the time.'

'It's common. But it's also debilitating. I have a question for you: when you were a young man, did you want to be independent of your parents?'

'Of course. I wanted to earn my own money, buy my own clothes and have my own place to live.'

'Were your parents pleased about your becoming self-sufficient? Or did they try to keep you at home?'

Howard laughed. 'They were delighted and proud that I wanted to make my own way! After being responsible for me for over 20 years, they were gratified that they had raised a son who could take his place in the world. After all, isn't that the whole point? Nobody wants to keep their child a baby forever.'

'Well, that's precisely the mindset that you should be applying to your business, too. When you think back across the last five years, have you viewed your business as a fragile thing that's totally dependent on you? Have you coddled it like a baby and wiped its nose every time it sneezed? Or have you tried to help it become self-sufficient?'

'I guess I've coddled it,' Howard said.

Joel returned to his chair. 'The problem with that approach is that if your business can't run without you, you don't really have a business, you have a job — with overheads! A business that truly serves your life is a business that has *a life of its own*, so that you have the freedom to choose how much or how little you want to be involved in it. That's what "breaking free" means. It doesn't mean getting out of your business or abandoning it, any more than your parents would abandon you. It's about *choice.'*

'I see your point,' said Howard, 'but you still haven't shed any light on how to get there.'

'You're right,' said Joel. 'Imagine that your new business is like a rowboat. You're the only person in the rowboat. To get where you want to go, you need to do everything yourself. You need to plot the course. You need to work the oars. You need to plug any leaks in the hull. If you don't do these things yourself, the boat will sink. Right?'

'Right,' said Howard.

'As you consider your future, you can choose to stay in your rowboat for your entire career. There's nothing wrong with that. Plenty of successful people enjoy rowing their own little boats. But you have chosen to become the captain of a big ship. You have employees and vendors and products. You have investors. Now, if you're the captain of the ship, can you afford to spend your time down in the engine room? Should you spend your time scraping the paint off the hull, or making meals for the passengers?'

'No, of course not,' said Howard.

'Right. As the captain of the ship, you need to do the big jobs that will ensure the ship and all its passengers travel safely to their destination. You cannot do everything. You need to empower your crew to do their jobs. You need to be able to go to your cabin at night, turn off the light and go to sleep knowing that the ship is in safe hands.'

'You're right – my decision to be the captain of a ship was a choice I made,' said Howard. 'I have a friend who writes novels. He has no employees. He has only himself and his computer, and he makes a very good living. He chose to row his own little boat. I've chosen to build a company.'

'The transformation from rowing a boat to commanding a ship doesn't just occur on its own, though,' said Joel. 'You need to intentionally design your business to run smoothly and profitably without having to fix every little problem and make every sale. You need to design it to run seamlessly, on time, all the time, like a well-oiled machine, even if you're not there. To use Michael Gerber's words again, this kind of business – the kind that works on its own – is called a *turn-key* operation. It's a business that becomes a true asset that others would buy. And it's the kind of business you need to create if you want to choose how you live your life.'

What Joel said made sense intellectually, but on an emotional level Howard wasn't so sure. He thought about the *Titanic*. On that cold April night, while the captain relaxed in the saloon, the crew steered the supposedly unsinkable ship into an iceberg.

'If you give employees too much responsibility,' said Howard, 'how can you guarantee that something bad won't happen? I have a friend who hired a general manager to run his business for him, and the results were disastrous. Every day the news is full of stories about employees who do terrible things right under their bosses' noses.'

'I can't speak about every example,' replied Joel, 'but it sounds like your friend made a common mistake. You can't just hand over the business to someone and expect them to run it the way you'd like. You still need to exercise keen oversight; but that's very different to doing everything yourself.'

'I think I understand,' said Howard.

'We've now covered the core philosophy that underpins effective business-building,' said Joel. 'If you don't mind, let's leave it here for today. I'm picking up the kids from school this afternoon, so if you're up for it, next time we meet let's work on applying this approach to your business.'

'When will that be?' asked Howard, surprising himself with his enthusiasm but also quietly envious of Joel and embarrassed that he never made time in his working day to pick up his kids. 'I'm flying to Hong Kong tomorrow evening but I could do an hour around noon.'

'That works for me,' said Joel. 'Twelve o'clock, here in the office. See you then.'

SUMMARY

BUSINESS-BUILDING PRINCIPLES

» The way you *think* about your business affects the way you *run* your business.

» Many business owners make a fatal assumption – that because they're good at doing the technical work of their business they can therefore create a business that works.

» To be successful, you can't just be a great *technician*; you need to be a great *manager* and *entrepreneur*, too.

» This means learning how to work *on* your business, not just *in* it.

» The aspects of your business you choose to work on depends on your goals.

» If your goal is to achieve more freedom, you'll need to design your business to run smoothly and profitably – with or without you.

» This kind of business is called a turn-key operation.

FREE RESOURCES: To download concise summaries, templates and resources to help you apply the principles in this chapter, go to www.mindfulentrepreneur.co/resources

THE FRANCHISE MODEL

At noon the following day, Howard and Joel resumed their conversation.

'To create a turn-key operation,' said Joel, 'it helps to follow one of the most successful, time-tested models. Michael Gerber calls it "the franchise prototype". It means that you view your business as the prototype for multiple franchises that are identical to the original. You intentionally structure your business so that you could recreate it anywhere and have each franchisee succeed.'

'I understand what a franchise is,' said Howard. 'But I don't think VinciWorks is a business that would lend itself to franchising.'

Joel explained that the franchise approach doesn't mean that you literally franchise your business. You simply act *as if* you were going to.

'There's a good reason for adopting this strategy for business management,' said Joel. 'Research shows that franchises are significantly more successful than typical start-up businesses. This is because a franchise is essentially a template for a self-sufficient, lead-generating, client-converting, customer-satisfying machine that almost anyone can pick up and operate.

'For example, whether or not you like McDonald's, the vast majority of McDonald's stores are successful. They operate over 35,000 restaurants in over 100 countries and territories around the world, employing more than 1.7 million people who serve 68 million customers each day. But here's what's interesting: a McDonald's franchise store averages $2.3 million in sales no matter who runs it or where it's located, and many stores have managers who are barely out of their teens.'

'How do they do that?' asked Howard.

'The answer is surprisingly simple: the company has set it up so that it's virtually impossible to fail. They have tried-and-tested systems for everything – from making burgers to marketing, recruiting and bookkeeping. The franchisee simply turns the key, opens the front door and it runs.

'When you begin thinking of your business as the prototype for a franchise, something incredible happens: you start shaping a business with such exquisite order and discipline that you could literally license the model to countless franchisees with full confidence that each would operate their individual business consistently and profitably.

'When you're done with your prototype, you'll have created a turn-key operation that can operate without you – regardless of whether you decide to open another location.'

SYSTEMATISE THE BUSINESS

Howard went to the window and looked at the rows of shops, offices and houses. His mind, which had been heavy with bleak thoughts, seemed a fraction lighter now.

He turned to Joel. 'Okay, Ronald McDonald, how do I create this turn-key operation in practical terms?'

'I thought you'd never ask,' said Joel, smiling. 'To transform your business into a franchise prototype, you'll need systems – lots of them. The secret to the success of franchised businesses is that they're *systems-dependent*, not *people-dependent*.

'Think about how things work in your business. Do you have defined, documented processes describing how each task needs to be performed, or do you simply expect your people to have the motivation and skills to figure out what needs to get done and to do it right each time?

'Further, is the knowledge of how to do what you do captured in a user-friendly operations manual, with a way to track that it's being followed, or does the knowledge reside in your head and the heads of your key people?'

Howard sat down behind his desk. 'Are you serious? Come on. We're not McDonald's. We're a small business with a lean staff. We have our ways of doing things that have been developed naturally, through trial and error, over time. Are these processes documented, tracked and written in a manual? No, of course not. No small business does that.'

'You're right, many don't,' Joel said, 'and that's one of the reasons so many small businesses fail to thrive. The reality is that most haven't systematised their operations. Systems are structured ways of performing tasks in order to achieve the desired results. And not having them in place is much more damaging than you might think.'

'Can you give me an example?'

'I can give you lots of examples. Let's take one from your own business. You said that cash flow was an issue. And you said it's because customers don't pay on time, right?'

'Right.'

'What does your current collections system look like?'

'I don't think we have a formal collection system. Our book-keeper follows up with the clients when invoices haven't been paid. She's been doing this pretty much since she started. It wasn't planned. I guess she just used her initiative.'

'Okay, let me put it this way: do you think the current process is optimised to bring in payment as efficiently as possible?'

Howard scrunched his forehead and thought for a moment. 'To be honest, I have no idea. I've always assumed it's our customers who are just slow payers, and I didn't want to upset them by chasing them too hard for payment. I thought it would make us look desperate. I suppose I've never really thought about collections as a distinct process in any meaningful way. Let me just call the bookkeeper and ask.'

'Please do,' replied Joel. 'But I hope you understand that the mere fact that you have to call your bookkeeper to ask her to describe the company's accounts receivables process proves my point. If VinciWorks were to become a franchise, you'd need to be able to clearly describe the accounts receivables system so that each and every bookkeeper in every independent VinciWorks franchise would know exactly how to apply it.'

After speaking on the phone to the bookkeeper for a few minutes, Howard hung up. 'The answer is that there is no collections process, and what's even more annoying is that she doesn't even think it's her responsibility to chase payments. She just enters the information into the books. As it turns out, it seems there are multiple people involved in the process, which isn't really a process at all. The sales reps chase payments because they want to get their commission, so they annoy the bookkeeper by asking if the invoice has been paid. But if there's no commission or if I'm the account manager for that customer, no one chases payment. Unless of course we're short of cash, in which case I ask the bookkeeper to speak to specific clients who have overdue invoices. No individual is ultimately responsible.'

'If key tasks like accounts receivable aren't deliberately designed and documented,' said Joel, 'you can't expect them to perform optimally. Unintentional or *ad hoc* systems produce unpredictable and unintended results. A business made up of random systems is successful only by chance, not by design.

'Franchises function differently. They install structured, designed, tried-and-tested systems for all functions of the business. They look carefully at each task and ask, "What's the best way to do this to achieve our goals?" Then they test it, and if it works, they systematise it so that anyone can do it the same way, every time with similar results. Nothing is left to chance.'

'Yeah, well, nothing here happens the same way twice,' said Howard. 'Every day when I walk through the door I feel like we're reinventing the wheel.'

'Let's imagine you're creating the ideal collections system from scratch then,' said Joel. 'Let's assume you have to do this because you've just hired someone whose job is managing accounts receivable. You have to train them. You have to be able to measure and evaluate their performance. You cannot rely on any prior knowledge they may have. You have to teach them everything, from absolute zero.'

'Honestly, I'm not even sure I'd know where to start,' said Howard.

'Start with the objective of the system. What results do you want it to achieve?'

'I guess it should collect money owed as quickly as possible. We need a healthy cash flow so the business can pay its expenses and continue to operate effectively.'

'Great. You said the system needs to get money in as quickly as possible. Every system needs an objective way to measure its performance. Can you identify what a reasonable performance standard might look like for your accounts receivable manager? For example, how many days are you willing to allow your invoices to be outstanding? Thirty days? Sixty days?'

'Ideally,' said Howard, 'there should be no outstanding receivables that are more than 30 days old. The exception would be if the client has been spoken to and we've negotiated a different payment date.'

'Okay, that's fair. Now let's consider the chronological tasks or steps that need to be taken to achieve that 30-day standard, including who's responsible for each step and by when they should complete it. The easiest way to do this is to draw a simple flowchart so you can visualise the process. Why don't you take a few minutes to do it now and then show me?'

Howard grabbed a sheet of paper from the printer and began drawing the flowchart. When he was done, he showed the drawing to Joel.

'It's rough and I doubt it's perfect,' said Howard, 'but it's got to be better than what's happening now.'

Gerschman, Finger, Goldman

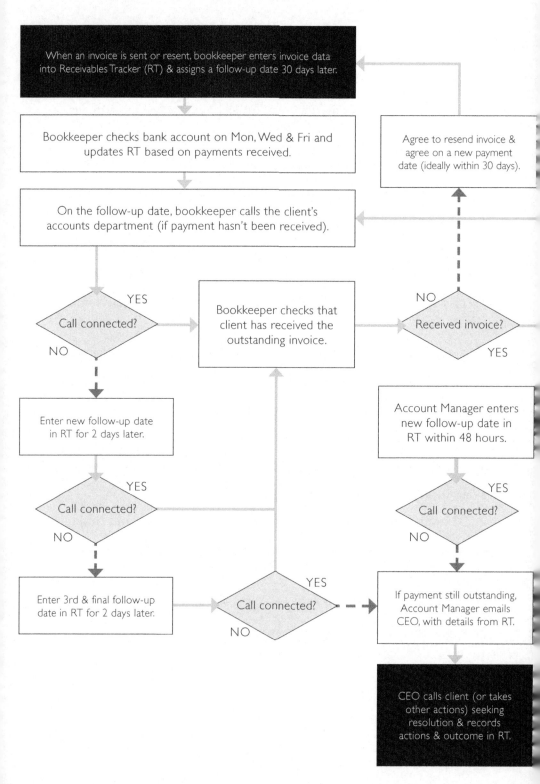

When an invoice is sent or resent, bookkeeper enters invoice data into Receivables Tracker (RT) & assigns a follow-up date 30 days later.

Bookkeeper checks bank account on Mon, Wed & Fri and updates RT based on payments received.

Agree to resend invoice & agree on a new payment date (ideally within 30 days).

On the follow-up date, bookkeeper calls the client's accounts department (if payment hasn't been received).

Call connected?
YES
NO

Bookkeeper checks that client has received the outstanding invoice.

Received invoice?
NO
YES

Enter new follow-up date in RT for 2 days later.

Account Manager enters new follow-up date in RT within 48 hours.

Call connected?
YES
NO

Call connected?
YES
NO

Enter 3rd & final follow-up date in RT for 2 days later.

Call connected?
YES
NO

If payment still outstanding, Account Manager emails CEO, with details from RT.

CEO calls client (or takes other actions) seeking resolution & records actions & outcome in RT.

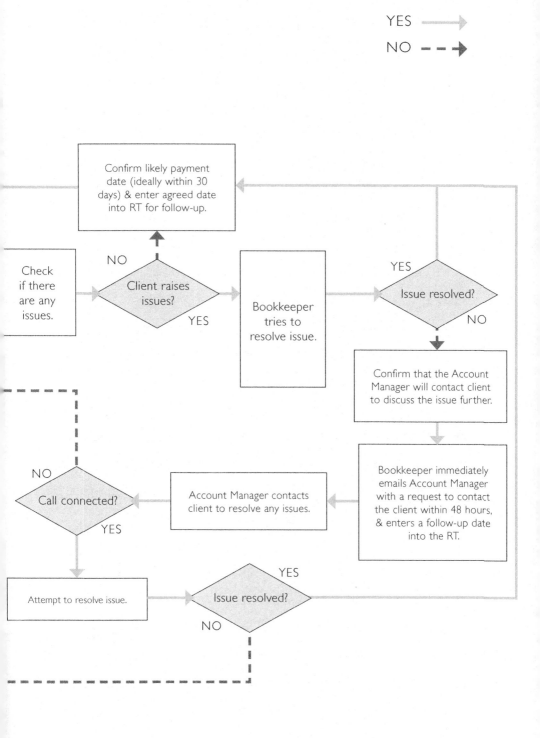

YES ———→

NO ----→

Confirm likely payment date (ideally within 30 days) & enter agreed date into RT for follow-up.

Check if there are any issues.

NO

Client raises issues?

YES

Bookkeeper tries to resolve issue.

YES

Issue resolved?

NO

Confirm that the Account Manager will contact client to discuss the issue further.

Bookkeeper immediately emails Account Manager with a request to contact the client within 48 hours, & enters a follow-up date into the RT.

NO

Call connected?

YES

Account Manager contacts client to resolve any issues.

Attempt to resolve issue.

YES

Issue resolved?

NO

Joel reviewed the system, questioning some of the steps in the flow and the feasibility of some of the timelines. Howard revised the system slightly, but was impressed with what he had been able to pull together in such a short time.

'Just two more things,' said Joel. 'First, what resources will your bookkeeper need in order to implement this system? For example, she will certainly need access to accurate invoice and payment information. She will also need to know who the Account Manager is for each client.'

'That's easy,' replied Howard. 'Our receivables tracker spread-sheet gets updated regularly as new invoices get sent. She already manages that document.'

'Perfect. Now, here's my second question, and it's critical: how might you track whether or not debtors have been followed up on time, as per the system? Without an effective mechanism to track how well a system is working, you'll never know if you're achieving your goals, and you may not be able to correct course before it's too late. With tracking mechanisms in place, you can quickly pick up issues before they become major problems.'

Howard replied that he didn't want to have to check constantly just to see if the system is being implemented. 'Wouldn't that defeat the whole purpose of having a system?'

'I agree,' said Joel. 'It has to be simple and efficient. In fact, in most cases, the person operating the system can actually track it for you. You said you already track invoice issue dates on your spreadsheet, right? Can you adapt that spreadsheet in some way?'

'We could put an extra column after the invoice date to indicate when the customer was last contacted,' said Howard. 'That way we could easily see which invoices are older than 30 days, and if the customer has been called. The spreadsheet columns could be sorted to show the oldest invoice dates on top. Once a week I could review it to check if there are any unpaid invoices that haven't been followed up. It would take only a minute to see how many are late, for how much money and when they were last contacted.'

'See, you're getting it,' said Joel. 'Now your task is to show this to your bookkeeper, compare it to what she's currently doing, make any helpful changes to the system based on her feedback, and ask her to begin implementing and tracking it. After 30 days, I'd be surprised if you weren't already seeing some results.'

'I'll give it a try and see if it makes a difference,' said Howard. 'You'll have to excuse me, though. You're probably going to spend time with your kids while I have a plane to catch. Welcome to my life! I'm leaving for Hong Kong. I'll see you when I return.'

'No problems at all, Howard. By the way, I know it's really a stressful time right now. If you want some extra strategies to help you stay balanced and focused, I think you'd benefit from speaking with a friend of mine. His name is Aryeh Goldman. He's an experienced counsellor and also happens to be a Rabbi. He's a special person; you'd like him.'

'Thanks, but I don't think I'm in need of a shrink just yet – or pastoral care.'

Howard's phone beeped as Joel shared Aryeh's contact details.

He also wrote Aryeh's number on a yellow sticky note and handed it to Howard.

'Just take his number,' said Joel. 'We both share the view that the state of one's business and one's state of mind are more deeply connected than you might think. Managing your internal state isn't just good for your overall sense of wellbeing; it'll also help you run your business more effectively. Think of it as part of our business building process.'

'Joel, you know that my priorities right now are business survival and growth. If you think he can help me in that arena, I'll consider calling him … if I can find the time. I have to go, but there's no reason *we* couldn't continue our process while I'm away. We don't need to be physically in the same room to do what we've been doing. There's a whole bunch of online meeting and collaboration tools we could use.'

'That's an interesting thought,' said Joel. 'I'm open to it. Feel free to Skype me to let me know how your new collections system goes while you're away.'

Howard left with a faint sense of comfort. He was sceptical that implementing one system would make a difference; nevertheless, it felt good to be working *on* the business not just *in* the business.

As his taxi crossed the Bolte Bridge heading towards the airport, the momentary comfort evaporated and the significance of this trip, and the all-encompassing stress, enveloped him once again. He called Andrea from the taxi, told her how much he loved her, and asked her to kiss and hug the kids.

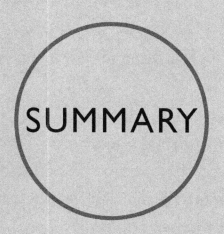

SUMMARY

SYSTEMATISING YOUR BUSINESS

» To create a turn-key operation, follow the time-honoured franchise model by thinking of your business as the prototype for multiple franchises just like it.

» The secret to the success of franchises is that they're *systems-dependent*, not *people-dependent*.

» Systems are structured ways of performing tasks in order to achieve the desired results.

» Unintentional or *ad hoc* systems produce unpredictable and unintended results. A business made up of random systems is successful only by chance, not by design.

» Create systems for each task in your business by defining the following for each system:

- A **title** (indicating the name of the system)
- An **objective** (explaining the result or outcome the system should produce)
- A **diagram** (a visual illustration of the system, using boxes and lines)
- The **tasks** (the key steps of the system, who's accountable and the timing)
- **Expectations** (performance standards, for example, timing, cost, quality, behaviour)
- **Resources** (the information, equipment or items needed to operate the system)
- **Tracking** (the way the system will be measured to ensure it's working)

FREE RESOURCES: To download concise summaries, templates and resources to help you apply the principles in this chapter, go to www.mindfulentrepreneur.co/resources

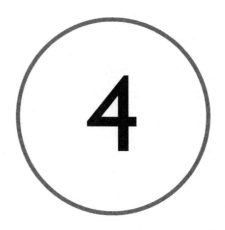

ARYEH AND THE
CORE PURPOSE

'Hi, Howard. Are you okay?' asked Andrea, concerned that he was calling her. His flight should have already left for Hong Kong.

'Not really. Everything has gone wrong. First, at the ticket counter I had to check the bag they usually let me take as extra hand luggage. Then I wanted to pick the short line to the gate but some idiot told me I had to join the longest baggage X-ray line in the history of airline travel. As result, I had to wait 20 minutes for a whole gang of unbelievably stupid teenagers who couldn't understand the most basic rules about 100-millilitre liquid bottles. Then the security people spent ten minutes searching both my bags for absolutely nothing. By the time I got through and into the lounge the Wi-Fi wasn't working and I couldn't get my emails. And, to top it all off, they announced that the plane has been delayed by at least an hour. I can't even work on my laptop because my battery needs charging and my power cord is in the bag they made me check in!'

Howard slumped in his seat. He was not a happy traveller. He was the archetypal road warrior. He flew over 120,000 miles a year. With loads of mileage and Cathay Pacific's top 'Diamond' status, he was accustomed to getting through check-in and passport control and directly into the lounge before most travellers have found their boarding passes.

Even his in-flight routine was perfectly choreographed: take-off, earplugs to avoid conversations with fellow passengers, work on his laptop, skip the in-flight meals, swallow half a sleeping pill, sleep for four hours, more work, prepare for landing.

This was a flight he had taken dozens of times before and he had hoped that it would be no different.

'That's so frustrating,' said Andrea. 'You land in Hong Kong early tomorrow and have a full day ahead of you. Why don't you close your eyes for an hour and get some rest?'

Howard was feeling tense and his mind was racing. Sleep might have done him some good, but it was about the last thing he was inclined to do.

'If you can't use your laptop, could you make any phone calls?' said Andrea, sensing that he didn't like her sleep suggestion.

'Joel actually gave me the phone number for some friend of

his. He's some sort of counsellor. I think he was worried about my stress levels. Maybe I should complain to him about Cathay Pacific!'

'That's not a bad idea. I've been worried about you too. I can hear how stressed you are.'

'Oh, come on. I wasn't being serious, Andrea. I'm just frustrated by the flight delay.'

'I think you should call. What have you got to lose?'

Howard knew he was experiencing extreme stress levels, even for him. Considering what had been going on, he thought he'd been handling things well. But he also knew that the business was not going to magically improve overnight, and that he would probably have to withstand this level of stress for quite a while longer. He said goodnight to Andrea and searched for 'Aryeh' in his Contacts. His flight wouldn't be leaving for at least another 45 minutes.

Despite feeling a little uneasy about it, he tapped Aryeh's phone number.

'Hi, Rabbi Goldman. This is Howard Finger. We haven't met before but a mutual acquaintance, Joel Gerschman, suggested that we should connect. Is this a good time?'

'Sure, Howard. And just call me Aryeh. I was hoping you'd call. I spoke with Joel earlier and he said that we'd enjoy talking.'

Howard was relieved that Aryeh sounded more like a friend than a doctor or psychiatrist.

'I'm at the airport and my flight has been delayed so …'

'You have some time to kill,' said Aryeh finishing off his sentence.

'Yeah, that's about right.'

'Joel briefly mentioned what you do. But why don't you tell me more about what's going on for you right now? I understand that it's a difficult time, right?'

'You mean aside from the fact that my flight was delayed, the battery has run out on my laptop and my power cord is in my checked baggage?' said Howard.

'That does sound frustrating. But I suspect that Joel's intuition to connect us was driven by something deeper than having your routine upset and running out of batteries.'

'Okay,' said Howard. 'For a start, I really don't know what I'm even doing here. I'm never at home. I don't see my kids enough. My business isn't giving me what it's supposed to give me, and I've just been told that I'm not actually running my business but my business is running me. So how would you respond to that?'

'It sounds like you're not happy,' said Aryeh.

Howard couldn't help but laugh. 'No, I'm not happy.'

'What's missing then?'

'What do you mean?'

'In my experience, when someone's unhappy it usually means there's something missing in their lives. Perhaps an important need isn't being satisfied.'

Howard gave a rueful smile. 'Well, let's start with the basics: money. I'm not making enough money. And it's causing everything else to fall apart.'

'Yes, money issues can very stressful,' said Aryeh. 'At the same time, I get the sense that there's more to it than just money.'

'With all due respect, right now having more money would make a huge difference to me and my company. Do you have a better solution for a guy whose business is facing bankruptcy?'

MASLOW'S HIERARCHY OF NEEDS

'I'm not a business expert, but I may know a thing or two about happiness,' replied Aryeh. 'Have you heard of *Maslow's Hierarchy of Needs*? It's been superseded by more recent theories, but I find that it's still a simple and helpful model for explaining what drives and satisfies us. It suggests that humans have four categories of needs, stretching from basic to high-level.'

Howard was surprised. He had expected Aryeh to offer ancient wisdom from some holy text. Instead, he was citing Abraham Maslow, a 20th-century American psychology professor. Howard sat up a little straighter in his seat and waited as Aryeh performed a quick search on his iPad, took a screen shot of a neatly typed list, titled 'The Four Categories of Human Needs', and sent it to Howard's phone. The list included the following points:

1. Survival and safety needs: food, clothing, shelter, security (most basic needs).
2. Social needs: participation, belonging, love, friendship, intimacy (slightly higher order needs).

3. Esteem needs: ego gratification, status, place in society (high-level needs).

4. Self-actualisation: the need to realise your potential by having a meaningful impact on the world (highest-level needs).

Howard scanned the list.

'Maslow's model suggests that each of these needs is critical to our happiness,' said Aryeh. 'But here's the secret many people don't understand: they're not all of equal importance.'

'What do you mean?' asked Howard.

'If you're a keen observer of human nature, you'll know that once our lower-order needs are met, at least to a basic degree, they stop affecting our happiness. There's a limit to how much food, clothing or shelter we need. Of course, we may *want* or *desire* more; we may (and often do) enjoy the immediate gratification of more. Yet once we reach a certain threshold, more doesn't make us happier.'

Aryeh told Howard about Princeton professor Daniel Kahneman who had conducted a study that proved this exact point. Kahneman asked respondents the question: 'Would you say that you are very happy, pretty happy, or not too happy?' Not surprisingly, those who earned more than $90,000 per year were twice as likely to say they were 'very happy' than those who made less than $20,000. However, there was little difference between the highest income earners and those who earned between $50,000 and $89,999 annually. Once their minimal income needs were met, more money didn't make them happier.

'Of course, we don't really need a professor to tell us that,' said Aryeh. 'We've all seen examples of wealthy people who seem to have everything but are deeply unhappy.'

'If I look at it objectively,' said Howard, 'I'm able to feed my family. They have shoes and clothes. And even though I struggle to pay the rent on time, we do have a roof over our heads. But as you can plainly hear, I'm not happy.'

'Exactly,' said Aryeh. 'While all humans require the lower-order necessities of food and shelter for survival, true fulfilment lies in the realm of our highest-order needs – the need for self-actualisation.

'Each of us has a deep need to realise our potential by living meaningfully. It constantly stirs within us until we respond to it, even if we're not consciously aware that it's happening. Sure, if you're literally starving, self-actualisation may not be top priority. But once you've met your basic needs, at least minimally, there remains a part of us that craves something deeper.'

OUR SEARCH FOR MEANING

'What does self-actualisation even mean?' said Howard. 'It sounds like psycho-babble to me.'

'Fair enough, it does. In fact, there are multiple views in the psychological literature about what it means. I simply think of it as engaging in meaningful activity.'

Aryeh told Howard about Viktor Frankl, a prominent 20th-century Viennese psychotherapist. His approach, called 'Logotherapy', inspired many of today's most powerful and popular psychological therapies and self-help approaches. In his bestselling book, *Man's Search for Meaning*, Frankl explained that many of us experience a void – a lack or inner emptiness – that can eat away at us. Its most benign manifestation is a feeling of boredom, but it can lead to depression, anxiety and addictive or escapist behaviours. He called it an 'existential vacuum' and believed it results from a lack of meaning.

'You're talking about an existential vacuum while I'm talking about cash flow, inept salespeople, stupid subcontractors and an unforgiving bank manager,' Howard said. 'My real and present problem is *cash*. Money represents the difference between solvency and bankruptcy. I don't have the luxury of worrying about meaning. This may be important to someone who has money and is bored, but that's not me. Give me the money and then let me get bored!'

'It's interesting you say that,' replied Aryeh as he read out a quote from Frankl.

For too long we have been dreaming a dream from which we are now waking up: the dream that if we just improve the socioeconomic situation of people, everything will be okay, people will become happy.

The truth is that as the struggle for survival has subsided, the question has emerged: survival for what?

Ever more people today have the means to live, but no meaning to live for.

— **Viktor E. Frankl,** *The Unheard Cry for Meaning: Psychotherapy and Humanism*

'You see,' said Aryeh, 'in my experience and that of my teachers, cash flow may be very helpful right now and it may relieve some of your current stress; I'm not denying that. But don't believe for one minute that cash alone will make you happy. Fulfilment comes when you meet your deepest human need: your drive for meaning.'

'That's way too deep for me. I'll tell you what basic need would satisfy me right now: a whiskey. Can you hold on a second?'

Howard wandered over to the lounge bar and poured himself a large single malt whiskey, with one ice cube. He noticed on the departures screen that his flight had been delayed again.

'Sorry about that. Do you still have time to talk?' asked Howard. 'I'm stuck here for at least another hour.'

'Sure, no problem,' replied Aryeh.

'Great, thanks,' said Howard. 'So what you're saying is that all I need to do is find meaning and everything will be hunky-dory. My business will become a success, all my bills will get paid and I'll live happily ever after.'

'No, that's not what I am saying. It's not some magic bullet. I'm not a businessman and I'm not giving you business advice; Joel can help you with that. But I'll say this, and if you take nothing else from our discussion, that's okay. Over the last two decades, a rapidly expanding body of research in the field of psychology has shown that meaning has a major impact on our happiness, mental health and our ability to cope with life's challenges – including the kinds of challenges you've experienced in your business. And when you're feeling happier, more resilient and better able to cope, you're more likely to have the focus and motivation required to run a successful business.

'There are a series of practices that can help us stay focused, balanced and motivated. But the first step is to work out what gives you a sense of meaning. How about we explore this together?'

'Well, I'm a prisoner in the Cathay Pacific lounge with nothing to do, so I'm open to almost anything.'

'Okay. Let's begin with your purpose.'

'I once had a purpose,' said Howard wryly.

'Oh really? What was that?'

'To get my golf handicap down to single figures.'

'Seriously, though, we often assume activities that make us feel good are therefore meaningful; but many activities only make us feel good temporarily. When you cut your handicap last time, you probably felt good for a short period of time; but how long did that feeling last?'

'Not long,' replied Howard. 'It was probably only a week later, after a bad round, that I was frustrated again. So are any activities truly meaningful then?'

'That's a good question,' said Aryeh. 'Empirical research has revealed some surprising truths. Playing a great round of golf, taking a hot bath, going on a holiday to Hawaii or watching your favourite TV show may be enjoyable, but those activities are all essentially focused on *you*, and thus don't usually create meaning.

'There's quite a bit of evidence that a paradox is at play here: it's usually when we *don't* focus on ourselves that we derive the most meaning and fulfilment. When you orient outwards, away from yourself, and focus on the impact you can have on others and on the world, you'll most often find meaning.'

'Interesting,' said Howard.

'Think of your own life. When do you feel most fulfilled? Is it when you focus on yourself – on your golf handicap – or when you create some great e-learning program that helps others learn something they might not otherwise have had access to? Meaning comes from doing something that reaches out and touches others in some way.'

'Aryeh, forgive me,' said Howard, 'but I'm not Gandhi or Mother Teresa. I'm not a do-gooder type. I'm a businessman who's just trying to survive.'

'I'm not suggesting that you need to be Gandhi, but the psychological literature is filled with studies to support the idea that fulfilment and happiness are linked to engagement in something meaningful, and meaning comes from doing something that reaches out and touches others in some way.

'Here's how Frankl put it,' Aryeh went on, reading the quote aloud:

The more you aim at it and make it a target, the more you are going to miss it … Happiness cannot be pursued; it must ensue, and it only does so as the unintended side effect of one's personal dedication to a cause greater than oneself or as the by-product of one's surrender to a person other than oneself. Then you will live to see that in the long run … [happiness] will follow you precisely because you had forgotten to think about it.

—Viktor E. Frankl, *Man's Search for Meaning*

'Okay, I get it,' said Howard. 'You're saying that happiness comes from engaging in meaningful activity that helps the world in some way.'

'Exactly. What's even more interesting is that by its very nature meaning is personal and unique. What's meaningful to you won't necessarily be meaningful to the next person. Which means that your task is to work out what's uniquely meaningful to you.'

FINDING YOUR PURPOSE

Howard took a deep breath and looked at the flight departure screen. He still had some time to kill. 'Okay. So if meaning helps to drive fulfilment — and can even contribute to my business success — how do I work out what's meaningful to me?'

'It's not difficult if you're prepared to stop for a few minutes and consider what's important to you in life, your values — and in particular, the ones that relate to the outward-focused impact or contribution you'd like to make.'

'And that's not difficult? I don't think I've ever done that formally.'

'If you're up for it, I can show you a brief exercise to help you think it through.'

'Well, I've got nothing to lose.'

'Great. I call the exercise "Finding your Purpose", although it's been called many names. Michael Gerber calls it your "primary aim" and your "dream". The motivational author Tony Robbins calls it your sense of "ultimate destiny". Michael Ray, another bestselling author, calls it your "highest goal". And Stephen Covey, who wrote *The 7 Habits of Highly Effective People*, calls it finding your "voice".'

'That's weird,' said Howard. 'It's the second time I've heard Michael Gerber's name in the last 24 hours. Joel mentioned him this morning. Have you read all the books you're quoting from?'

'Yes, I've read them all,' said Aryeh.

'All right, I'm in your hands. Where do we start?'

'Have you got a pen and something to write on?' asked Aryeh.

'Sure,' said Howard as he reached for his black notebook and Sharpie pen.

'Okay, this may sound a bit strange at first, so take a deep breath,' said Aryeh. 'Imagine you've just died and you're present at your own funeral, looking down on the gathering of relatives and friends.'

'That sounds grim.'

'Just try it. It's not so bad; assume you've lived a very long and fulfilled life. Your children, grandchildren and great-grand-children have come to bury you. One of your grandchildren gets up and starts to pay tribute to you and your life's accomplish-ments. Now write down what you would like them to say. Take your time with it.'

'Could I work on this for a little while and call you back?' asked Howard.

'No problem. I'll wait for your call.'

Howard put the phone down, took a swig of whiskey, pulled the notebook closer and wrote:

Howard Finger did much and experienced much. Everything he did, he did with passion and completion. He experienced many things people only fantasise about. He travelled the world, walked the Inca trail, lived in the Amazon, drove to Tierra del Fuego and visited all the wonders of the modern world. He lived in countries in every continent and in several of the world's major cities. He had amazing kids whom he loved and engaged with and who loved him – the coolest of all the dads! He main-tained an amazing marriage. He achieved a black belt in karate, ran a marathon, became a partner in a law firm in Hong Kong and senior vice-president in a public company, and built his own company from nothing to £100 million.

Twenty minutes later Howard called Aryeh to share what he had written.

'That's impressive,' said Aryeh. 'But keep going; I'll wait on the phone for you. Most of this is about your personal achievements. What would your grandkid say about your impact on others? Isn't that important to you, too?'

'I guess so. Okay, I'll continue.'

My granddad was a nice guy, a fun guy, always smiling, always generous and always positive. (Well, almost always.) He lived life fully, extracting the greatest amount from every moment. He saw good in everyone. He hated gossip and lived with an intensity in this world that belied the likelihood of another. He touched people's lives wherever he lived and gave massive value to lots of people. With integrity, he tried everything and judged no one. He created new, innovative business models that created and supported communities both virtual and physical in a way that made them sustainable, allowing people and businesses to grow and interact in new, open and honest ways. Forthright and brutally honest, he offered no excuses. He had a dry and wicked sense of humour. He wanted to know himself and the truth about life, the universe and everything.

'Okay, I'm done,' said Howard as he read what he had written to Aryeh. 'But it's a jumble of ideas. How will I convert this into a coherent purpose?'

Over the next hour, Aryeh and Howard discussed what Howard had written, highlighting key words and phrases that seemed significant, before distilling those key words and phrases into a few core themes. For example, Howard recognised that recurring words like 'new', 'created' and 'innovative' represented a key theme in his life: his deep desire for creative expression. Similarly, Aryeh pointed out how phrases like 'allowing people and businesses to grow', 'touched people's lives' and 'supported communities' seemed to reflect his desire to help others and contribute real value to their lives.

As Howard and Aryeh worked through the other significant words and phrases, they noticed additional themes. Words like 'greatest' and 'massive value' hinted at Howard's desire for large-scale impact. The words 'grow' and 'sustainable' signified his value of creating ongoing, sustainable value – teaching others *how* to fish, rather than just giving them fish – while phrases like 'forthright', 'brutally honest' and 'no excuses' summed up his attitude to life.

'Okay,' said Aryeh, 'now see if you can wrap those themes together into an easy-to-remember catch phrase – a bit like a slogan for your life.'

Howard worked on it and came up with:

Create the greatest sustainable value – no excuses!

As he read it out loud, he felt like he'd experienced a moment of realisation, an epiphany. And in a quiet undertone said to himself, 'So *that's* what I'm about.'

'That's pretty powerful,' said Aryeh. 'It expresses your desire to be creative and to help others in a large-scale, sustainable way. How does it feel?'

'I like it. It feels like it fits. I'm just a little unsure what to do with it now.'

'The idea is to express it in every aspect of your life – at home, in your business, everywhere.'

'Does my business really need to express my purpose?'

'Well, it depends on you. If you're happy to run a business that simply doesn't conflict with your purpose, that's fine. Many people do. And they try to find meaning in other areas of their life. But if you want to run a business that inspires, energises and fulfils you because it actually makes a difference to the world, then aligning it with your purpose is worthwhile. Is that what you want?'

Howard considered before answering. 'It seems daunting trying to live a life and run a business that's focused on creating the greatest sustainable value – no excuses! But it is inspiring. While I'm still painfully aware of my financial problems and other responsibilities, in a way it gives me some perspective on what's really important.'

Over the airport loudspeakers came the announcement that the flight was finally boarding for Hong Kong. Howard thanked

Aryeh for what was certainly one of the longest and most interesting phone calls he had ever made. As soon has he hung up the phone, Howard shifted into road-warrior mode and headed towards the plane.

SUMMARY

YOUR CORE PURPOSE

» Once our lower-order needs – like food and shelter – are met to a basic degree, they stop affecting our happiness.

» Fulfilment lies in the realm of our highest-order needs: the need for self-actualisation and living meaningfully.

» When you feel happy and fulfilled, you're more resilient, better able to cope and more likely to have the focus and motivation required to run a successful business.

» We experience most meaning when we focus outward, on our contribution to or impact on others.

» Meaning is personal in nature, so you need to identify the impact or contribution that is specific to you.

» Use the 'Finding your Purpose' exercise to help you identify the unique impact you want to have:

- Write your 'eulogy' by considering what you hope people will say about you at your funeral;

- Scan what you wrote for the most important words or phrases and circle them;

- Look for common ideas in the circled words or phrases;

- Group any common ideas into key themes; and

- Identify a central idea, word, phrase or sentence that integrates each of your themes.

FREE RESOURCES: To download concise summaries, templates and resources to help you apply the principles in this chapter, go to www.mindfulentrepreneur.co/resources

THE CORE
BUSINESS PURPOSE

Create the greatest sustainable value – no excuses. As the train sped between the green hills of Lamah Island, through the shipping container terminals and over the steel bridges that connected the airport to the Kowloon mainland, Howard pondered how he could use his core purpose to convince his friends (and VinciWorks shareholders) Rick and Gordon to help him solve the cash-flow issue.

Upon arrival, he exchanged pleasantries and then began to explain the difficulties the business was facing. His friends asked question after question, quizzing him on the numbers. Finally, after a long silence, Gordon leaned forward and said, 'Howard, let's cut through all the crap. The bottom line is whether the business is really worth saving.'

Howard paused and as he considered his response, an image of his future grandchild proudly eulogising his granddad crossed his mind. For the first time since asking his friends to invest, he found himself talking about the business with genuine passion.

'Things are obviously tough right now, and I know we're at a crossroads. But I also believe that this is a genuine opportunity to refocus on building a more successful business.'

'What makes you think you can change things?' asked Gordon.

'All this time, I've been caught up working *in* the business, rather than *on* the business. I've never had the time to step back and think about how to grow it strategically. Instead, I'm spending all day every day putting out fires.'

'Why should things be any different now?' asked Rick.

'I now know what I need to do. I need to systematise the business, with documented, step-by-step procedures for all tasks, like franchises have. I can then delegate those tasks with confidence that things will run consistently and efficiently. That way, I won't have to do it all myself, I won't have to be continually putting out fires and I'll have more time to work on stabilising, improving and growing the business. In fact, I've already started by implementing a system for managing receivables.'

'It sounds good in theory, but the unpaid receivables and the cash-flow problems make me hesitant to reinvest,' said Rick. 'I don't want to throw more good money after bad. But I am pleased to hear the passion back in your voice, Howard. Let's meet again tomorrow to discuss strategies for putting out the most immediate cash-flow fires. And, depending on what we come up with, we'll confirm whether or not we'll invest more funds.'

Howard left the meeting and headed back to the hotel. On the way, he checked his email. There was a message from Natalie, his bookkeeper, confirming that she had implemented the new collections system. Following the system, she had called a number of clients with overdue accounts. Three of them told her they were pleased that she had called and agreed to pay their overdue invoices before the end of the week.

It turned out that the invoice payment authorisation often got 'lost' on the partner's desk. Natalie's follow-up call prompted the person in the client's accounts department to call the partner and get the authorisation signed and processed. Three simple phone calls and an additional £35,000 would be in the bank by Friday. The immediate bills could be paid. With a smile on his face, Howard sent a short email to Joel, telling him the good news and thanking him for the collections system.

Back in the hotel room that evening, Howard searched online for 'factors affecting happiness'. Without reading it properly, he clicked the first link. It took him to www.marketinvoice.com, a new online marketplace where invoices could be 'factored' through an online auction site. Buyers would bid against each other and offer to essentially 'buy' your unpaid invoices at discounted prices.

Howard filled in a form, and within a couple of hours became the first Market Invoice client to factor invoices issued to legal firms. Together with the new receivables collection system, within 24 hours he'd been able to bring in enough cash to extinguish the hottest cash-flow fires, including paying enough to the subcontractor so they could settle their VAT bill, pay that month's staff salaries, and even pay some of the overdue school fees.

The immediate pressure was off, and that night Howard slept well for the first time in weeks.

THE CORE PURPOSE OF A BUSINESS

After waking in the morning with the words 'no excuses' ringing in his head, Howard met again with his shareholders, Rick and Gordon. He told them that overnight he had fixed the most immediate cash-flow problem. They were impressed. Responding to Howard's initiative, as well as to his renewed focus and enthusiasm, they agreed to lend the company more money.

It was time to go home. Howard boarded the plane and settled into his usual aisle emergency-row seat. However, instead of plugging in and working, he sat back, closed his eyes and started to think about his core purpose.

Early the following day, direct from the airport and before Joel came into the office, Howard emailed his team about the impact of the new collections system and dealt with the most pressing emails. Upon Joel's arrival, even before he had made his coffee and sat down at his desk, Howard thanked him again for the collections process and told him about his conversation with Aryeh. He showed Joel a sheet of paper with the words: 'To create the greatest sustainable value – no excuses!' printed in big bold letters.

'That's amazing,' said Joel. 'It fits well with our process. We started with the company's collections system because I wanted to give you something that would deliver immediate value and address an urgent need. But Aryeh is right. To truly build a long-term, sustainable and fulfilling business, you need to start at the beginning. And that means defining the purpose.'

'But I just showed you my core purpose. What do you mean?'

'I'm talking about a purpose for the *business*,' replied Joel. 'Your personal purpose should align with the purpose of your business, so your personal reflection was perfect. Now let's try to create the same level of clarity about why your business exists.'

'Hang on. The purpose of my business is to generate enough profit to pay my bills and support my lifestyle, isn't it?'

'That's one aspect. But your business also needs an outward-focused, meaningful purpose in the same way that your life needs one. Put simply, your business should be squarely focused on delivering some worthwhile benefit to the people it serves – your customers and stakeholders. While specific goals, such as making a certain amount of revenue or profit, are critical, they should be driven by a more fundamental, underlying business purpose.'

'You've lost me,' said Howard. 'I get why I need something like this for my personal life, but why does my *business* need a purpose?'

'Let's take a step back for a moment. Think about it this way: a business will only succeed if it first fulfils an important function or purpose for its customers, right?'

'Yes, I suppose that makes sense. If I don't deliver sufficient value to satisfy the needs of my customers, I'm not going to sell very much, to many people, for very long.'

'Would you agree then, that if fulfilling that important purpose for customers was *the* crystal-clear, universally understood purpose of the business, you and your team would be more focused on the right goal – namely, satisfying customers?'

'Yes, I suppose,' said Howard. 'Focus is always good.'

'And would you also agree that if you and your team were exclusively focused on satisfying customers, you'd be more likely to build a bigger business and generate more money from happier customers, who would then refer more customers?'

'Okay, okay, I get the theory. But do businesses really do this?'

'The best ones do,' said Joel. 'They do it for another reason, too. It's not just about satisfying customers; it's about finding a purpose, something to stand for – something beyond profit. Customers prefer, trust and rally behind businesses that stand for something worthwhile and important.'

'Now you're starting to sound like Aryeh,' said Howard.

'I'm okay with that,' said Joel. 'We're in good company. Take Apple. Their "Think Different" campaign – the one that helped launch their exponential growth – is a perfect example. Their first campaign TV ad featured a line-up of world-leading scientists, artists, creative thinkers and activists – people who changed the world in some positive way because they were willing to think outside the box – to "think different". It tapped into people's desire to create positive change, to make a difference, to think creatively and differently. Deep down many of us want to make a difference, even if we're not doing it right now. In his book, *Start with Why*, Simon Sinek expressed it powerfully. He said that when you buy an Apple product, you're not just buying a beautiful, well-designed piece of machinery. In a sense, you're buying the ability to change the world. You're starting to "think different". You're connecting with Apple's underlying purpose, and that's inspiring. Almost 20 years later, the loyalty that Apple's purpose generates among its fan base is still strong and hard to replicate.'

Joel explained that there are many more examples of companies that have a powerful purpose:

- Google: To organise the world's information and make it universally accessible and useful.
- Walmart: We save people money so they can live better.
- Marriott Hotels: To make people who are away from home feel they are among friends and really wanted.
- Disney: To make people happy.
- Starbucks: To inspire and nurture the human spirit – one person, one cup, and one neighbourhood at a time.

'That's a pretty amazing idea that savouring a simple cup of coffee has the power to connect people and create community,' said Howard.

'Yes, I agree,' replied Joel. 'The founder of Starbucks, Howard Schultz, saw his highly profitable global business as an expression of that important business purpose.'

'There is no doubt that deep down, I want to make a difference in the same way as Apple, Starbucks and Disney have done; but they're big companies who have the power to make a difference. Can it really be the same for a small business like mine?'

'Yes,' said Joel. 'For example, a fire and electrical maintenance specialist I work with determined that his company's purpose was "to protect life and property". Protecting or saving just one life is surely a meaningful way of making a difference in the world. I also work with an IT services company that serves medical professionals; their purpose is to "empower people to do important work". And I know a childcare centre whose purpose is "to create the leaders of tomorrow". I could go on.'

'I see,' said Howard. 'They're all working towards a larger, more meaningful purpose.'

Joel nodded. 'And there's another benefit, too. A timeless purpose inspires ongoing motivation. When you feel like you're doing something important, you're more motivated. If you're someone who wants to impact the world in a positive way, if you hope to leave a lasting legacy of some kind, if that ideal lies at the heart of your personal core purpose, then only an inspiring business purpose will truly call forth your energy, passion and commitment. And when that happens, your effectiveness will skyrocket, too.'

Howard thought about his epiphany in the airport lounge when he'd first formulated and articulated his personal core purpose.

'There are many examples of this throughout history,' said Joel. 'Military theorist Carl von Clausewitz and Chinese military general Sun Tzu both observed this phenomenon in even the most extreme of contexts. In times of war, soldiers who are passionate about their cause fight harder. They turn the world on its side. They stop at nothing. Bring this into your business and see what happens.

'And if your staff feel as though they're working towards something bigger, something important, they'll also be more motivated and more productive. Of course, it's your job to continuously reinforce the link between what your staff do day-to-day and your underlying purpose; but when you do, the impact can be enormous.'

'Okay,' said Howard, 'I get the value in defining a business purpose and I understand that it should somehow be an expression of my personal core purpose. But how do I actually determine the core purpose of the business?'

'Let's do that now,' said Joel. 'We'll apply a strategy called "the five whys". You simply start by describing the product or service you provide, and I'll keep asking, "Why is that important?" until we arrive at a core purpose.'

'All right,' said Howard. 'Let's start.'

Here's how the exchange went:

Q: How would you describe your product or service offering?

A: We provide compliance software.

Q: Why is compliance software important?

A: Companies have to be compliant or risk being fined or going to prison.

Q: That might be the reason customers buy your products. But why is compliance important in the first place?

A: It ensures people and businesses comply with the law. For example, by ensuring that businesses comply with the *Proceeds of Crime Act* and the Anti-Money Laundering Regulations, it makes it harder for criminals to hide the proceeds of crime or to clean dirty money. This also makes it harder to finance terrorist activities, which helps to stop terrorism.

Q: Why is that important?

A: It ultimately makes for a safer, fairer and more honest world.

'It doesn't get much more important than that, does it?' said Joel. 'It only took four questions, but I would say that's the underlying purpose of your business. If you agree, write it down.'

Howard wrote it across the top of the whiteboard that hung behind his desk. Stepping back, he read it aloud. 'Our core purpose is to make a safer, fairer and more honest world. Wow, no one could argue with that. And you know what? It's actually true. It resonates with me and with what we do.

'I know we have lots of work to do to implement the systems necessary to get the house in order,' continued Howard. 'I also know that our contribution to creating a safer, fairer, more honest world may be humble. But for the first time in years, I'm excited to drive the business forward. What I need to do now is go to London and re-enrol both Josh, our COO, and Nigel, our UK managing director, into this purpose and get their commitment to systematise their departments.'

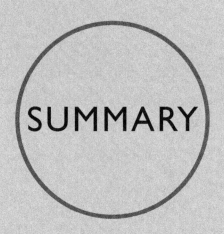

SUMMARY

YOUR BUSINESS PURPOSE

» Your *business* needs a meaningful purpose in the same way that your *life* needs one.

» To be successful, you and your people must be focused on fulfilling a valuable purpose for your customers and stakeholders.

» Customers prefer, trust and rally behind businesses that stand for something worthwhile and important.

» A timeless purpose inspires ongoing motivation and boosts effectiveness – yours *and* your team's.

» To uncover your business purpose, apply the 'Five Whys': ask why your product or service is important up to five times until you reach a core reason or purpose.

FREE RESOURCES: To download concise summaries, templates and resources to help you apply the principles in this chapter, go to www.mindfulentrepreneur.co/resources

REFUSAL OF THE CALL

After a 22-hour flight, Howard landed in London and went straight to his accountant's office in New Bond Street. The firm's senior partner was an old friend and was there to greet him when he arrived. Nigel, the UK managing director, got there 20 minutes late but it did not dampen Howard's mood.

He opened the meeting with enthusiasm, stating that he had experienced a major breakthrough. He appreciated that things had been tough recently, but he had raised some money from the shareholders and intended to relaunch the business with an entirely new management approach and a new core purpose statement:

VinciWorks' purpose is to create a safer, fairer and more honest world.

Nigel held up his hand, motioning for Howard to stop talking.

'Howard, with all due respect, the problem is not the management approach,' said Nigel. 'I've conferred with the others and we all agree that the real problem is *you*. You're not around on a day-to-day basis and your salary and travel costs are a drain on the cash flow. Bottom line: we feel we can do a better job without you.'

In a state of shock, Howard looked to his accountant for support. None was forthcoming.

Nigel explained that he intended to take over the running of the business as the CEO. He would position Howard as chairman instead of CEO, and the team would call on him to engage as and when they felt he could offer value.

At this point, Nigel put a piece of paper in front of Howard. 'You need to sign this. It documents and confirms that you will arrange for VinciWorks to issue shares to me and Josh for the additional responsibilities that we're now willing to undertake.'

Howard's stomach churned and a sour taste rose in the back of his throat. He hesitated. 'So this is an official ambush, is it?'

'Of course not,' replied Nigel. 'We're simply trying to save the business. But if you don't sign, then you can assume that Josh, me and the rest of the team will immediately resign.'

At some level, Howard was sure that Josh wouldn't conspire in this way, and there was a moment when he could have dug deep, called Nigel's bluff and refused to sign. But the risk of having to run the business without Nigel and Josh felt too great. He was trapped, and all his energy and inspiration dissipated. He felt like he was back in the schoolyard having his bag taken by the bullies while everyone laughed at him. He started to think that maybe Nigel was right. Maybe he *was* the problem.

Still reeling, Howard fell back on his legal training and without intending to be strategic, recognised that he could not sign the document as drafted because he didn't have the authority to commit on behalf of the shareholders. Instead, he edited the letter, committing to 'use his best endeavours to get the shares transferred'.

He stood up. In a daze, he walked out of the office and onto New Bond Street. He headed down to the London Underground to catch a train straight back to the airport. While waiting for the Cathay Pacific ticketing staff to find him a seat on the next flight to Melbourne, he received a text message from his daughters asking him to bring home some duty-free perfume. Knowing that his credit cards were full and he couldn't even buy a bottle of perfume for his kids, he almost started to cry.

AWARENESS AND INTERPRETATION

Sorting through his bag, Howard came across the yellow sticky note with Aryeh's phone number. On an impulse, he decided to call.

'Hello?' said Aryeh.

'Hi, it's Howard Finger. I'm the one who called you from the airport when my flight was delayed.'

'Howard! It's good to hear from you. How are you? Are you living your core purpose?'

'Funny you should ask that. I'm probably as far from it as I have ever been.'

'You don't sound great. What's happening?'

'I'm in London. I've just been ambushed by my managing director, who told me to get lost, resign as CEO and hand over a load of shares. He'll now run the business without me. So much for living my core purpose. Seems to me my core purpose is to fail at whatever I try to do.'

'Howard, I really feel for you. That must be tough. Is there anything I can do to help?'

'I doubt it,' replied Howard. 'It seems I'm just destined to fail. It's the story of my life. And I'm wondering if it's a life worth living.'

Aryeh paused for a moment before responding. 'I'm not trying to downplay what you're going through. I can only imagine your disappointment after all you've invested. At the same time, obstacles are a normal part of the journey that all of us go through in life – and the "work" domain of our lives is no exception. It certainly doesn't mean that you're a failure.'

'I realise that obstacles will arise, Aryeh,' said Howard. 'I don't expect it to be smooth sailing all the time. It's just that I was inspired and motivated to pursue my purpose, but instead of support, I got beaten up by the very people who are supposed to support me

– my senior management team, my employees, even my friends and professional advisors, like my accountant. It's hard not to give up. I'd rather fall under the plane than get back on it.'

'I'm not saying that I know the "right" move for you to make in this situation,' said Aryeh. 'So I'm not going to tell you what to do. What I do know, though, is that your next move will require careful consideration and for that you'll need to be in a balanced state of mind. If you're open to it, I can share some ideas with you that may help you cope with what's happened and regain your composure so that you can make a sound decision about your next step.'

'Go on, I'm listening.'

'Well, last time we spoke, we said that becoming aware of your core purpose is a critical foundation for living a meaningful, fulfilling life. But, as you've experienced, challenges will arise along the way, sometimes knocking you off course. Sometimes we're able to bounce back from such setbacks pretty quickly. On other occasions, the stress, pain or disappointment can stop us in our tracks, holding us back from moving forward productively.'

'That's exactly what it feels like right now.'

'Yes, I can hear that. Which is why I'd like to share some helpful insights into how our minds work. Consider it a crash course in human psychology.

'There are four key steps to work though: (1) Uncovering your story; (2) Testing the story; (3) Fostering a growth mindset; and (4) Opening to opportunity. We'll start by trying to uncover the story you're telling about this situation. Allow me to be controversial for a moment. I think the ambush isn't what's made you so upset today.'

1: UNCOVERING YOUR STORY

'Well, why else would I be upset?' asked Howard.

'I'm exaggerating to make a point,' Aryeh said. 'What I mean is that it's not *only* what happened today that's causing your reaction. Events themselves are only part of what triggers our emotional and behavioural responses. There's actually an intermediate phase between the time you experience an event and the time you react emotionally. It's the reason ten people can experience exactly the same event but have ten completely different reactions.'

'Are you going to share what that phase is, or are you keeping it a secret?' asked Howard.

'Yes, yes, I'm getting there. You see, when we experience an event, it gets processed or filtered through our minds. We tell a story about that event, we make assumptions about it, we interpret it in some way – and it's that interpretation or story that sparks our reactions. This process is often subconscious and can be almost instantaneous; but make no mistake, our stories can deeply shape our emotions and behaviours.

'What's so interesting is that the way we tell the story – our interpretation of events – is often strongly shaped by our past experiences and unique personalities. Which is why we all respond so differently to life's events.'

'I'm not sure I get it. I'm not making up stories. I was ambushed.'

'Okay, let me put it differently. In his book, *The Success Principle*, Jack Canfield expresses this idea with a simple but powerful formula: *Event + Response = Outcome*. In other words, whether we like it or not, challenging events will occur in our lives. But our emotions, behaviours and ultimately the outcomes we experience aren't simply a result of those events. They're profoundly affected by the way we respond to or interpret what has happened. We tell a story about the events in our minds — and that makes all the difference.

'Take your situation. The ambush — and request for your resignation as CEO — was the event that occurred. We can also appreciate the possible outcome: you're experiencing intense disappointment, to the point that you're wondering whether to throw in the towel. Right?'

'Yes, that's about right.'

'But as we said, there's an intermediate variable: the way you've *responded* to or interpreted the event. I'd like to uncover that story because the outcome hinges on it. What is it about what happened today that's leading to your current feelings?'

'Well, my instant answer is that I got shafted and it hurt, but presumably you mean something deeper. I guess I'm assuming they think I'm not cut out for the job. I'm not good enough. In essence, I've failed as a CEO.'

'I imagine it would be upsetting to feel that,' said Aryeh. 'But tell me more about why this is knocking you off balance. Sometimes, for example, current events can be linked to larger stories from our pasts that add to the emotional charge.'

'I guess it's just another example of not being good enough.'

'What do you mean?' asked Aryeh.

'I've been told I'm not good enough all my life, right back to when I failed the "11Plus", my final year of primary school exam. Or even before that, when I wasn't picked to play in the soccer team; or when I was seven and the big kids, the school bullies, grabbed my schoolbag and refused to give it back. There are lots of stories and I guess they are all pretty much the same.'

'As hard as this might be for you, Howard, this is a critical insight. Can you see how it wasn't just the event in isolation that triggered your emotional response? You've refracted it through the lens of a story that you've been telling all your life. It's your "I'm not good enough" or "I'm a failure" story. No wonder this latest episode is having such a powerful effect on you.'

'But surely anyone would be upset if they got ambushed and kicked out of their own company – even without a backstory?'

'Sure they would. But it might not have the same kind of hold over them. Everyone gets upset, feels stressed and experiences dis-appointment. But when the pain stops us from bouncing back and makes you question the point of your existence, it's worth exploring how your mind is interpreting the situation. This awareness – or mindfulness, as I like to call it – is an essential first step to managing your emotions.'

'I don't know. I'm still a bit confused.'

'Let's demonstrate this with a quick thought experiment,' said Aryeh. 'Imagine you were just ambushed, exactly as it happened. But this time you interpret the event as follows: "I'm experienced, capable and skilled in this field. Right now, my colleagues think they can run the business better than I can and want me to resign. I don't happen to agree, because I think there's much I can still offer. But resigning may give me the time and space to contribute in a more strategic and influential way, which is really where my strength lies. It may also give me more time with my family." Now how would you react emotionally if that was your story?'

'I'd probably still be disappointed because I wanted to lead the company towards unbridled success. But I suppose I wouldn't feel crushed in the way I do now.'

'Right. And what would you do next if that *was* your story?'

'I certainly wouldn't give up. I'd probably just take a day or two to regain my composure, plan my strategy and set up a meeting to discuss what happens next.'

'See the difference? You can experience the exact same event, but the way you interpret it can affect everything – how you feel about it, what you do next and whether you're open to any new opportunities that may arise as a result.'

'Okay, I get it now. Becoming more aware of the story I'm telling is important because it influences how I feel and act. But what if I really am a failure? I can't just play Jedi mind tricks with myself all my life by changing my story when I feel like it. I have to face reality.'

2: TESTING THE STORY

'Great question. It's also a good segue to step two, which is about *testing* your story. If your story is likely to lead you *away from* rather than *towards* your core purpose, it can help to gently reality-test or challenge the story before you accept it as truth.

'Research shows that when we hit a challenge and our emotions rise, our stories can often become exaggerated or blown out of proportion. Today's upsetting scenario can call to mind lots of unrelated – but in our minds damning – evidence of past failures. Likewise, it's easy to slip into catastrophic thinking about the future; a specific, limited event can, in our minds, snowball into an ominous future disaster. A little reality-testing can often shrink events to a more realistic size, making them more manageable and less likely to knock us around. For example, are you absolutely, 100 per cent sure you're a failure?'

'Well, I've been told so many times. And as you can plainly see, my business isn't exactly a roaring success right now.'

'Okay. You're a lawyer by trade, Howard, so imagine you're now a lawyer for the opposing side. What evidence in your life might support a different interpretation?'

As Howard considered Aryeh's question, he recalled his days as a lawyer arguing on behalf of clients. 'Now that you mention it, after failing to get top grades in my final year of high school, I still managed to get into law school, successfully complete the degree and eventually become a partner in a leading international firm.'

'That's already impressive. But keep going. What other evidence can you think of?'

'I built, managed and grew globalsources.com, enabling my previous employer to go public on the NASDAQ.'

'Anything else come to mind?' asked Aryeh.

'Well, I've written and published a book, earned a black belt in karate, travelled the world for a couple of years and created two beautiful children.'

'Hmm … you don't sound like a failure to me. How does that fit with your failure story?'

'I guess the failure story isn't entirely accurate. I have failed, but I've also succeeded.'

'Right. That's a much more accurate and balanced way to perceive yourself. And you'll find that when you're thinking in a more balanced way, it takes the edge off strong emotions. You might not be happy about the situation, but reality-checking your story can help you feel more balanced and respond with more composure.'

'Even if what you're saying is true and I'm not a complete and utter failure, the fact remains that my career is all but over. I'm basically out of a job and I'll have no way of feeding my family. How do I deal with that reality?'

'Again, let's test it. You know more about your situation than I do. Were you actually fired? Or are they simply asking you to resign as CEO? Do you have to accept their request?'

'I don't technically have to accept Nigel's request, but even if I can convince the directors and shareholders to support me, it may mean losing Nigel and Josh. And it would be extremely difficult for me to run the business from Australia without a UK sales team and without someone to run the back office.'

'Are there any other options?'

'If I hand over the reins, there's a chance I might need to take a cut in salary. But maybe not. Now that I think about it, Nigel mentioned wanting me to stay on as chairman. Perhaps I could agree to step down as CEO but stay on as chairman on the condition that they continue to pay me. In some ways, this wouldn't be such a terrible outcome, provided they do a decent job of running the business. It would free up time to spend with my family and think about strategies to help build the business.'

'It sounds like there are at least a couple of ways in which you could handle this situation.'

'I suppose so. But neither will be easy.'

'That's right. This process isn't about pretending that everything will be simple and easy. It's about gaining a more accurate perspective on reality – so you can regain your balance and your ability to make wise business and life decisions.'

'I see what you're saying,' Howard said. 'And surprisingly, I actually feel a bit less stressed already. But there are only so many setbacks a person can handle. What if this keeps happening?'

'I don't know how much you can handle, Howard. Only you can know that. But whenever someone tells me about their many setbacks, it reminds of a wonderful quote from the famous basketball player, Michael Jordan:

I've missed more than 9000 shots in my career. I've lost almost 300 games. Twenty-six times, I've been trusted to take the game-winning shot and missed. I've failed over and over and over again in my life. And that is why I succeed.

'I'm no Michael Jordan,' said Howard. 'He was one of the greatest sportsmen of all time.'

'Perhaps not. But he had something we can all acquire. It's called a *growth mindset* – and it's step three in our process.

3: FOSTERING A GROWTH MINDSET

'Challenges in business, and in life, can destabilise even the best of us, shaking our identity and sense of self. It's particularly so when the challenges come thick, fast and from all sides. In such cases, even reality-testing our stories may offer only small relief.'

'So what can help?' asked Howard.

'While we can't control the challenges life throws at us, we can respond like Michael Jordan and make a crucial mindset shift that improves our ability to accept the situation, remain balanced and learn from it. And that's precisely what shifting from a *fixed mindset* to a *growth mindset* is all about.'

'I'm listening …'

'Let me share some fascinating research with you. Professor Carol Dweck of Stanford University conducted a study on how kids cope with failure. She asked kids to attempt a range of puzzles that progressed from easy to very hard. As the puzzles became more challenging, many of the kids grew frustrated, disengaged and eventually gave up. But some didn't. Actually, they became *more* energised as the challenges increased. Why?

'After talking to the kids, Dweck found that those who gave up more quickly assumed that their puzzle-solving capacity was a fixed trait. They did fine on the easy puzzles, but when they started to struggle they said to themselves: "The first puzzles showed I was smart. Now these harder puzzles show I'm simply not up to the task." So they gave up rather than continue to face their deficiencies.

'The kids who persisted, on the other hand, assumed their puzzle-solving ability was a flexible trait that could grow and develop. In fact, they saw struggling with tough puzzles as precisely the challenge they needed to improve. They weren't discouraged by failure; they didn't even think they were failing. They thought they were learning.

'Don't underestimate the implications of this for you and every other business person. People with *growth mindsets* tend to bounce back sooner. They see a setback as an opportunity to grow and they intensify their efforts as a result. It's no wonder they're more likely to succeed.'

'So if I focus on learning, I'll eventually slam-dunk like Michael Jordan?' said Howard.

'How tall are you exactly?'

'I'm a tall five foot seven inches.'

'I don't know about dunking like Jordan then. There are still limits. But I do know that the latest research in the field of neu-roplasticity shows that many of our traits are more elastic than we might have thought.'

'All right, so what do I do with this whole growth idea? It's a nice concept, but how do I apply it, especially when I'm in the middle of a challenge, like right now?'

'As with any new mindset or skill, it takes practice. Here's an exercise for you. You've just experienced a major challenge in the form of an ambush. A fixed mindset might say: "I'm a failure. I'll never be a good CEO. I might as well give up." But imagine, for a moment, that this event was designed as part of a training program to help you grow. What have you learned from the ambush?'

'Perhaps I shouldn't be so trusting of others' intentions,' said Howard.

'Okay, what else have you learned?'

'It's certainly made me reconsider my role. Joel has been talking to me about handing over the day-to-day activities and focusing more on strategic growth. Perhaps this is the just the push I need to make it happen. And I suppose it's also given me the chance to learn the coping skills you've shared with me today.'

'Great observations. That took you all of a minute. And as with any new skill, the more you practise it, the easier it becomes to test your thinking and view challenges in terms of what you can learn.'

'Aryeh, I really appreciate your time. It's been a very helpful conversation. I don't know if I'll be able to implement it all but I'll give it a shot.'

'I'm glad it's helped. Before you go, though, there's one last step. Sometimes there are situations that seem bleak, even after reality-testing and growth-thinking. In those cases – in fact, in *all* cases – it helps to be open to opportunities. More often than we might imagine, new opportunities arise from what seem like negative situations. But we only recognise them as opportunities if we're open to seeing them. Otherwise they can easily pass us by.'

'It sounds almost mystical or spiritual to me,' said Howard.

'I do happen to see things from a spiritual perspective. There's an old Jewish saying that applies to challenging situations: "Even this is for the good". I think of my life as a journey, with highs and lows, challenges and opportunities. And when obstacles arise, I believe that they're designed to help me create a better reality. I've experienced it many times. But you don't necessarily have to see it from a spiritual vantage point. Even from a purely practical perspective, deciding to see challenges as potential opportunities means that you're more likely to look for them, see them and tap into them when they arise.'

'I guess that makes sense. What opportunities do you think my situation will offer up?'

'I think you've already recognised several. Now you just need to stay open and act on the best of them. And keep me posted on how you go. I'm happy to talk whenever you need.'

Howard thanked Aryeh again and hung up. He was still upset but the conversation had taken the edge off. He began thinking about his options. He could fight the challenge to his leadership and try to regain control. He could give up altogether and simply resign. Or, instead of making any drastic decisions just yet, he could step back from the daily business grind for a while, think about how 'even this is for the good' and consider what other opportunities the ambush might have revealed.

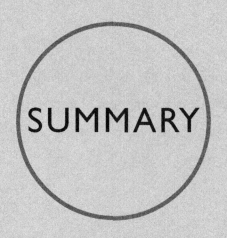

SUMMARY

INTERPRETATION

Life is full of challenges and obstacles

When obstacles cause stress, pain or disappointment that throws you off balance, apply four key steps to help you regain your composure and make wise decisions:

» **Uncover your story**

- Whenever we experience an event, our minds interpret or tell a story about the event. This story profoundly affects our reactions and outcomes.
- Becoming *aware* of the story you're telling enables you to address it.
- Ask: what story am I telling?

» **Test the story**

- Our stories can often be exaggerated or blown out of proportion.
- Gently reality-test your story before you accept it as truth.
- A little prodding can often shrink events to a more realistic size, making them more manageable and less likely to knock us off balance.
- Ask: what evidence might support a different interpretation?

» **Foster a growth mindset**

- People with growth mindsets tend to bounce back sooner, viewing setbacks as opportunities to grow and learn.
- Ask: what can I learn from this situation?

» **Be open to opportunity**

- Often new opportunities arise from what seem like negative situations.
- Deciding to see challenges as potential opportunities makes you more likely to look for

them, see them and tap into them when they arise.

- Ask: what opportunities might arise?

TESTS, ALLIES
AND ENEMIES

Having given it a lot of thought, Howard decided to take a step back and let go of any meaningful day-to-day engagement in VinciWorks. The first few weeks were liberating. He had more time to spend with his family and more time to work on his golf. He even began to explore other possible business ventures, at least in concept. But soon enough, staff members began to contact him, seeking his advice, input and assistance. It started with a trickle but quickly became a steady stream. He tried to direct them to Nigel and Josh. But eventually even Josh began seeking Howard's input and complaining about Nigel.

The financial results did not improve. In fact, they deteriorated.

Without being directly involved day in and day out, Howard was able to gain a more objective, bird's-eye view of the business. The problem wasn't just poor results. The problem was even more fundamental: there was no strategic direction, no targets to measure progress against and no visibility in terms of cash flow, income or expenses. There was no way to really know what was going on financially. And without real-time insight into how the finances were tracking, there was no way to truly 'manage' the business. Joel's words about working *on* the business rather than *in* the business resonated loudly.

Within three months, VinciWorks was all but imploding. Nigel called Howard to say that to keep things afloat he, Josh and Howard would have to take pay cuts. In fact, Nigel admitted that even with those measures, the business might not survive. But with revenues dropping fast, something had to be done.

Howard called his shareholders in Hong Kong.

'I handed things over in good faith, but the situation is getting worse not better,' he told them. 'Either Nigel is killing the business or the business itself is now so flawed that it's probably not worth saving. I need to do something.'

'Howard, the shareholders have always trusted you,' said Rick. Somehow he always sounded composed, even in the midst of chaos. 'I think you should fly to London and take back control – at least for the next six to 12 months. This will give us enough time to decide whether to shut down the business or build it back up.'

'Unfortunately, it's probably also time to let Nigel go and use his salary to help keep the business afloat,' suggested Howard's other co-director, Gordon. 'In 2008, when the global financial crisis hit, you fired staff and hunkered down to see if we could survive. It seemed to work then. It may be our only option now.'

Psychologically and emotionally, it had taken a lot for Howard to pull back. Now he would have to dig deep, and go back into the fray.

Before boarding yet another flight to London, he called Aryeh for some moral support.

'Hey, Howard. Good to hear from you. How's the sabbatical?'

'The business is a disaster and I've been asked by the directors to go to London, fire Nigel and take back control.'

'Ah, another call to action. Deep down, this is what you really wanted all along, isn't it? You said you felt as though you hadn't finished the job.'

'I know. It's just that I'd almost come to terms with my new role and now ...'

'Now you get to give expression to your core purpose,' said Aryeh.

For a moment, Howard was taken aback. In deciding to step away from the day-to-day running of the business, he'd also relegated his core purpose to the deep recesses of his subconscious. What good was a purpose that could never be fulfilled? But as he let Aryeh's words sink in, he knew this was exactly what he wanted, however difficult it might prove to be.

Howard landed at Heathrow at 5.30 a.m., went to the office briefly to collect his thoughts and prepare, and then met Nigel at the Starbucks nearby.

'Hi, Nigel.'

'Nice to see you, Howard. Welcome back. Can I get you a cappuccino or maybe a croissant?'

'Let me get them,' said Howard. As he waited in line, he wondered how Nigel could appear so calm and cheerful. He surely knew this was going to be a difficult conversation.

'Look, I'll be straight with you,' said Howard as he sat down with the coffees. 'Our financial position is not good, as you said yourself the other week. The business has deteriorated, and at a faster rate since you took control. I gave you the opportunity but things are just not working and we have to make some changes before it's too late.'

'I know, Howard. And I've been working on it. I have a solution that will solve our problems. I've found some people who want to buy the business.'

This was the first Howard had heard of, or even thought of, a sale. Was this another ambush? Incredulous, he asked, 'Really? Where did this come from?'

'Believe me, you're going to be eternally grateful to me for this. It's our only way out.'

'Nigel, I'm not going to sell the business at a fire-sale, bargain-basement price,' said Howard. 'We may be in a difficult spot right now, but I'm not going to just give VinciWorks away. I should have taken back control last time I came to London. That was my mistake. But I'm ready to step back in now and work on building a great business.'

'Hold on a second. Are you saying you're not interested in selling? I've found you a way out. No more struggling with cash flow, more time with your family. I thought this would be your dream come true.'

'Potentially, but it really depends on the offer.'

'They haven't given me a number yet,' said Nigel. 'But their pre-condition is that they want me to stay on as CEO.'

Intimations of a conspiracy arose in Howard's gut, but he held his anger at bay. 'Given how far revenues have fallen, a standard valuation won't net us enough to make a sale worthwhile. So you can tell your buyers that if they want to buy VinciWorks, a "reasonable" offer will be too low. They'll need to make an "unreasonable" offer. They'll need to pay a premium.'

'My understanding is that the buyers have a much bigger plan in mind, and VinciWorks is just one small but important part of it,' said Nigel. 'They want us because we already have most of the top law firms as clients, we have a ten-year track record with recurring revenues and we have instant credibility. This is a strategic play for them, so I'm pretty sure they'll pay a decent premium. What do you want me to do?'

'Tell them I'm not interested in playing games. If they want the business, they'll need to put an offer on the table within seven days. After that, I'll start to reintegrate myself as CEO.'

'Where does that leave me if you're back in as CEO?' asked Nigel.

'I have a plan but I don't see any point in discussing it if we're going to receive an offer that includes you staying in place as CEO. So until then, it's a moot point.'

Within days, an 'unreasonable' offer was received. The buyers valued the business at three times what Howard considered to be a 'reasonable' offer. The deal would mean that Howard would personally receive £1 million in cash. Although in his gut he didn't want to sell, even at that high price, accepting the deal would allow him to cease the crazy travelling, spend quality time in Australia with his family and have enough money to create something new. A Heads of Agreement was executed by the parties and the sale was scheduled to be completed prior to Christmas – a mere 90 days away.

The buyers made it a condition, and a part of the due diligence process, that Howard clean up the financials and prepare a complete and comprehensive five-year business plan, after which a final purchase contract would be drawn up and signed.

At the airport heading home, Howard phoned Aryeh to fill him in on the day's events.

'Wow. It sounds almost too good to be true,' said Aryeh. 'You should be thankful. It seems like a miracle.'

'Yes, I guess so,' said Howard. 'The money is good, but for some reason I'm a little unsure. As I've said to you, I still feel like I'm walking away before the job is done.'

'You said you still have a couple of months while you complete the due diligence process and write the business plan, so it sounds like the job's not quite over yet,' said Aryeh.

Howard immediately called Joel to ask for help in writing the business plan – and for some guidance on what to do next in his life.

THE BUSINESS PLAN

Howard arrived back in his Melbourne office and launched into a meeting with Joel.

'Okay, so you need a business plan for the buyers. The best way to do this is to write it as if you were actually going to apply it to your business. That way, it will be authentic and real.'

'Do I really care? Why can't I just give them a fairy story?' Howard said.

'Because if they have any business experience and acumen, they'll see right through it. It won't be convincing.'

'All right, I suppose we can make the plan as realistic as possible. Where do we start?'

'There are two fundamental components to an effective business plan,' said Joel. 'First, you need a clear sense of what you want your business to become. I call this your Strategic Direction. Then, you need a well-considered plan of attack for how you're going to get there. I call this Strategic Execution. If either one of these is missing, your chances of success diminish significantly.'

'That sounds like business jargon to me.'

'Okay, fair enough; I don't like jargon either. Think of it this way: it's almost impossible to create an effective plan of action if you don't know where you're going. Do you remember the conversation between Alice and the Cheshire cat in *Alice in Wonderland*? One day Alice came to a fork in the road and saw a Cheshire cat in a tree. "Which road do I take?" she asked. "Where do you want to go?" replied the cat. "I don't know," Alice answered. "Then," said the cat, "it doesn't matter [which road you take]."'

'This sounds a bit like Aryeh's conversation about meaning and direction.'

'I'm not surprised. It's the same idea, just applied to business. But it's also important to realise that even a clear, inspiring vision is worthless without a practical action plan to make it happen. And that's what an execution plan is all about. Does that make sense?'

'It does. So hit me: how do I do it?'

'There are ten key components to a comprehensive business plan. The first half is about direction and the second is about execution. Let me draw it for you.'

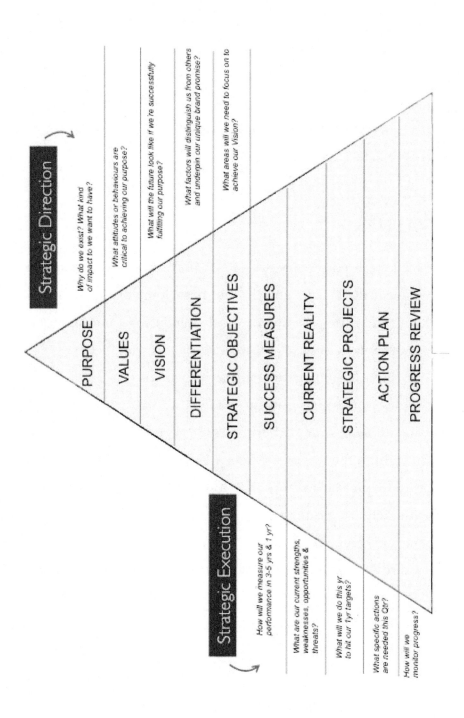

Strategic Direction

PURPOSE — Why do we exist? What kind of impact to we want to have?

VALUES — What attitudes or behaviours are critical to achieving our purpose?

VISION — What will the future look like if we're successfully fulfilling our purpose?

DIFFERENTIATION — What factors will distinguish us from others and underpin our unique brand promise?

STRATEGIC OBJECTIVES — What areas will we need to focus on to achieve our Vision?

SUCCESS MEASURES — How will we measure our performance in 3-5 yrs & 1 yr?

CURRENT REALITY — What are our current strengths, weaknesses, opportunities & threats?

STRATEGIC PROJECTS — What will we do this yr to hit our 1yr targets?

ACTION PLAN — What specific actions are needed this Qtr?

PROGRESS REVIEW — How will we monitor progress?

Strategic Execution

Howard studied the picture. 'Hang on, the first one is purpose – haven't we done that already?'

'Yes, we have. So you know what kind of impact you want the business to have. You want to *create a safer, fairer and more honest world.* Everything else flows from this purpose. We can now jump to step two, which is values.'

VALUES

'While your purpose explains *why* your business exists, your values represent the beliefs, attitudes and behaviours that are essential to fulfil your purpose. Think of them as enduring, fundamental ways of operating, regardless of the circumstances,' said Joel.

'How is defining this going to help me? Isn't it just theoretical?'

'If your values end up being a set of theories that sit in your office drawer, gathering dust – I agree, they're a waste of time. But if they serve as practical guidelines for your day-to-day attitudes and behaviours and those of your people, they can be extremely powerful. Whether you're aware of it or not, the way you and your staff think and act on a daily basis creates the culture of your business. And while many leaders don't proactively seek to shape their culture – they see it as something that "just happens" – the best leaders proactively define and nurture their desired culture.'

'I hear people talk about culture all the time, but you still haven't explained how it will help grow the business,' said Howard.

'Because having the right culture is critical to growth. Ever heard the phrase, "Culture eats strategy for breakfast"?'

'No.'

'It means that your ability to implement strategies to grow and differentiate yourself is dependent on the way you and your people think and act, the way you treat your customers, the way you collaborate with each other, whether you care about excellence and quality, the way you adapt to change, and so on. In short, you need to define your culture proactively – otherwise it will define you.'

'Okay, so values set attitudes and behaviours, which in turn drive the implementation of strategy. That's clear. But how do I define my company values?'

'Let me give you a few examples first and then some questions to guide you. An important but often unstated value is "care" or, as I like to call it, "going beyond". It's demonstrated by your people voluntarily taking a personal interest in the customer's situation and proactively helping out wherever they can.

'Another value that I know you rate highly is "trustworthiness". Staff who value trust will provide honest, sincere and customer-focused advice. Empowering your staff to think for themselves and use their initiative to overcome problems is often referred to as "adaptability", while the value of "innovation" tends to drive the proactive improvement of internal efficiencies and therefore improve the customer experience.

'I've also heard you express pride in your staff when they perform high-quality work. The value of "quality" also tends to drive referrals and secure renewals. Another common and key value is "collaboration" which manifests in staff working as a team. Personally, I highly value "professionalism", which is expressed in staff being organised, punctual and responding to communications in a timely manner.

'Those are just examples though,' Joel continued. 'You'll need to decide on your values based on what's important to you and your business. I recommend you limit it to between five and eight values. Any more and it will be too difficult to focus on and remember day-to-day.'

Joel wrote two key questions on the whiteboard to spark Howard's thinking: what are the guiding beliefs or attitudes that are crucial to achieving your business purpose? What behaviours do you expect to see, regardless of the circumstances?

Howard took the whiteboard marker and, after some to-ing and fro-ing, he agreed on the following: Quality, Innovation, Service, Honesty, Proactivity, Fun, Growth, and Professionalism – no excuses.

'Great. Would you say that you currently operate according to these values?'

'I can't say that they're front of mind at all times, but I certainly hope I live by them.'

'What about your staff?'

'I guess we all know that growth is critical to keeping ahead of the game, but we don't really do anything to foster this as a value. I've been thinking about signing up our people to some online courses to keep building their skills and help them grow personally and professionally, but I haven't done anything about it yet. On reflection, I suppose it's unrealistic to expect the values to be upheld when I haven't explicitly communicated them.'

'That's exactly the reason it's so critical to define, demonstrate and communicate the values of your business. You can't micromanage everything people do. But if you can instil some fundamental values into the culture, you're more likely to get staff to think and act in ways that align with those values and your expectations.

'You can also use your values as a recruitment tool to screen candidates. You want to hire people who share your values and are therefore more likely to fit your culture from the outset.'

'Okay, so let me summarise to make sure I understand,' said Howard. 'Purpose is about the impact I want my business to have. Values are how we need to think and act to achieve that purpose. Right?'

'Exactly. I think we're ready for step three.'

VISION

'Have you thought about your vision for your business?' asked Joel.

'I thought it was to create a safer, fairer and more honest world?'

'That's your purpose – why you're in the business in the first place. Your vision is what the future will look like if you're successful in fulfilling your purpose. It answers the question: where do you want to be in three to five years?'

'I know in general terms that I want to make money and satisfy my customers. But how can I see what's going to happen in three to five years?'

'You can't. But you can think strategically about how you would *like* the future to look. You can set ambitious but realistic goals. And when you know what you're aiming for, you can focus your energy on trying to achieve it.'

'That reminds me of when Aryeh asked me where I was going with my life. I guess you're asking me where my business is going. And if I don't know where it's going, how can I expect to get there? Maybe that's why I feel like I'm constantly going around in circles.'

'Right. A Harvard study illustrates this point. Researchers conducted a survey in which they found that only 3 per cent of that year's graduating class had thought about and documented their career vision. Another 12 per cent had thought about their vision but had not taken the time to write it down. The rest, a staggering 85 per cent, had not seriously considered their goals beyond graduating with an MBA.

'The same group was resurveyed ten years later. The survey found that the smallest group, the 3 per cent who had documented their vision, was generating *ten times* the income of the largest group who hadn't considered it. They concluded that by documenting your vision and tracking your progress, you have a 300 per cent better chance of reaching it.'

'They're pretty good odds! So what do I do?'

'There are three critical components to your vision:

(1) Defining your niche; (2) Assigning a "stretch goal"; and (3) Setting a "time horizon". Let's start by defining your niche.'

1: DEFINING YOUR NICHE

'I think I understand this already. My niche is providing online risk and compliance learning and management tools.'

'That's partially correct. Your product or service offering is one component of your niche. But there's more to it. Your niche is actually the intersection between *who* you serve (your customers), *what* you offer (your products or services) and *where* you'll offer it (your geographic scope). Tell me who you sell those products or services to and where.'

'Who do I sell to? Well, most of my clients are large law firms.'

'That's a good answer. Many clients I work with answer: "Anyone I can sell to!" One of the secrets to success in today's market is to operate with laser-sharp focus on a particular customer group, often called your target market. Think of it as going narrow and deep rather than broad and shallow. Like a laser beam, your contracted focus enables you to direct your precious energy and resources towards reaching a particular customer group and deeply meeting their unique needs in ways that others can't. Trying to be everything to everyone is a recipe for mediocrity.'

'That sounds right; I think I've always known that intuitively. But what about Apple and Facebook? What's their laser-sharp focus? They both seem to be targeting the entire world.'

'They are now. But both those companies started with specific target markets. Apple focused on computer geeks and Facebook focused on university students. And they built from there. It's wise to achieve success with one market before you break out beyond it. So the fact that you have a specific market focus is a good thing – at least to begin with.'

'To be honest, I can't say that I deliberately targeted the legal market. I started with banks in Hong Kong, as I had an existing relationship and reputation with them. But I went out for drinks one evening with my ex-partners from the law firm and they said, "If you're building e-learning for banks, why don't you do it for our annual mandatory Continuous Professional Development [CPD] training?" I said, "Sure, why not." They said, "On second thoughts, you'll never get the Hong Kong Law Society to accept online CPD training." We bet a case of Chanson Montrachet that I could convince the Law Society. It took me 18 months but I won the bet!'

'Nice story. So first time it was more luck than deliberate strategy. This time let's rely on more than just luck.'

'You could call it luck. But Aryeh would say there is no such thing. It's just being open to the opportunity.'

'What?'

'Never mind.'

'Okay, I have another question about your niche. Where are your law firm clients located? Geography is the third component.'

'We started in Hong Kong, but many of our clients are now

global and most have their head offices in the UK.'

'Okay, let me summarise it,' said Joel, '"VinciWorks provides online risk and compliance management and learning tools to large law firms mainly in the UK but also in Hong Kong and other parts of the world." Is that right?'

'Basically, yes.'

'So that's where you are now. But what niche will you be focused on in three to five years?'

'How do I decide that?'

'Let's create a simple niche matrix to help us analyse it. First, list all your products and services down the left-hand side of the board, including any products or services you don't currently offer but may want to in the future. Does that make sense?'

'Well, yeah. In fact, I was thinking about offering consulting services as an add-on to our risk-management software. We end up educating the client anyway, so why not charge for it?'

'That's exactly the kind of strategic thinking you need to be doing.'

Howard listed all his current and future products and services.

'Good work. Now along the top of the page, list the various customer groups you currently serve as well as those you could serve in the future. Just list them broadly: for example, large UK law firms.'

'What do you mean by customer groups?'

'It's important to group together potential customers with similar characteristics. You're looking for groups of people or organisations who are most likely to buy your products or services. Then you can select which groups to target first.

'Consider two broad types of customer characteristics. First, there are demographic similarities, like industry, speciality, number of staff, revenue, location. Or, if you're selling to consumers, there's gender, occupation, education, income level, social class, marital or family status and ethnic background. And second, there are psychological similarities, like values, aversion to risk, behaviour, personality, attitude, lifestyle or interests. You could use both these categories to help you identify customer groups.'

'I think I need an example.'

'If you're starting an art gallery with expensive, unique pieces, for example, people under 18, with little disposable income living at home with their parents, won't be a likely target group. On the other hand, wealthy, retired or semi-retired baby boomers living in affluent neighbourhoods, who have a taste for aesthetics, may be a very lucrative market. And so might younger, 30- to 40-year-old, high-flying executives who want to portray an image of success and culture. Do you get the idea?'

'Okay, so in my world, I guess it's professional service providers like lawyers, accountants and bankers who all have compliance requirements and can potentially go to prison if they don't comply.'

'Great. Those are three customer groups: lawyers, accountants and bankers. But you need to be more specific. Is it *any* lawyer or only large law firms?'

'Right now, based on our premium price points and course content, it's only larger law firms. But I guess we could create new courses and price them to suit smaller firms – or even accountants and bankers.'

'You're getting the idea. Start listing your customer groups and remember to consider their geography.'

Howard listed them all.

MARKETS ➡ PRODUCTS/ SERVICES ⬇	Top tier law firms (UK)	2nd & 3rd tier law firms (UK)	Legal services (Europe)	Legal services (USA)	2nd, 3rd & 4th tier accounting firms (UK)	3rd & 4th tier banks (UK)
Off the shelf online compliance training						
Bespoke online training						
Learning management system						
Risk management						
Risk consulting						

'The next step is to evaluate your customer groups to determine the ones to focus on first. Let's look at each one in terms of a few factors: how profitable they are, how accessible they are, how many there are (that is, the market size), the extent of competition in the market and the degree to which they align with your business purpose. Just write number 1 in the box that best meets these criteria, number 2 in the next best fit and so on.'

'To be honest, I don't even know which groups are most profitable,' said Howard.

'Don't worry; that will be part of your homework. For the moment, just give your best guess.'

'At a gut level, it's probably not the very biggest clients. It's the tier-two clients who aren't as demanding and don't have as many support issues due to the smaller number of users, but who are still willing and able to pay full price. The tier-one clients give us credibility and marketing benefits more so than profitability. And in the legal market, we've somewhat saturated tier one. So tiers two and three might be the way to go. There are lots of them, and once you get them they're easier to support.'

'And with the credibility and experience you've earned in the legal sector, there's no reason you can't also break out into the other sectors you mentioned, like banks and accountants.'

'Yes, you're right,' said Howard. 'And in those markets, maybe the second, third and fourth tiers would be also a better or easier place to start.'

Howard continued to work on the boxes, refining the target

markets and prioritising them.

MARKETS ➡ PRODUCTS/ SERVICES ⬇	Top tier law firms (UK)	2nd & 3rd tier law firms (UK)	Legal services (Europe)	Legal services (USA)	2nd, 3rd & 4th tier accounting firms (UK)	3rd & 4th tier banks (UK)
Off the shelf online compliance training	1	7	2			
Bespoke online training						
Learning management system		6	5			
Risk management		4	3			
Risk consulting						

'That's great, Howard. You've now identified your current niche and new areas to move in to. How does it feel?'

'Great – *if* I was still going to be running the business,' said Howard, reminding himself that the plan he was getting excited about was not for him to execute. 'You know, this is the first time I've had some clarity around our direction and how I could grow the business – and now I'm selling it. There's a part of me that would really like to implement this.'

'I understand. Either way, though, you need to complete the plan, so let's keep moving. The next step in refining your vision is to determine the ambitious, measurable result you'll achieve if you're successful in this niche. I call this your "Stretch Goal".'

2: ASSIGNING A 'STRETCH GOAL'

'Are you asking me to predict the future, based on the markets I highlighted in the table?'

'Yes, but in one powerful sentence that's really engaging and easy to grasp.'

'That sounds simple!'

'Just give it a go,' said Joel.

'How about: "To provide outstanding customer service and products that delight our customers?"'

'A good start, but it needs a more specific, measurable finish line, so you and your team can know when you've achieved the goal. Think of JFK's 1961 stretch goal "to send a man to the moon and return him safely by the end of the decade".'

'Can you give me some business examples?' asked Howard.

'Sure. You can have quantitative, numerical targets like amount of revenue, or number of customers; or qualitative targets that are a bit more subjective, like being number one, most popular, the best. In 1950, Boeing set a goal to become the dominant player in commercial aircraft and bring the world into the jet age. Microsoft wanted to put a computer on every desk and in every home using great software as an empowering tool. Heinz set out to be the world's premier food company, offering nutritious, superior-tasting foods to people everywhere. Mattel aimed to be the premier toy brand, today and tomorrow. I could keep going, but you get the picture.'

'Okay, how about: "To generate £1 million in revenue"?'

'Not bad,' said Joel. 'Just be careful, though. If you set a revenue target, be certain it'll inspire and motivate your team, even when you're not there. Would a revenue target do this for your team considering they won't be directly sharing in the profits?'

Howard thought some more. 'How about this: "VinciWorks will provide innovative online compliance training, risk-management software and consulting to at least 60 per cent of the top 1000 UK law firms and 500 of the UK's third- and fourth-tier accounting and banking businesses." We already represent about 150 of the top 300 law firms in the UK and the goal extends our market into the banking and accounting sectors.'

'I really like it. It's clear, specific, measurable and engaging. It would be a real achievement. So you're going to focus primarily on the UK?'

'Yes, I think we have a great opportunity to grow in the UK professional services market, which is big enough on its own to challenge us. Trying to break into Europe or North America would be expensive, distracting and too risky right now.'

3: SETTING A 'TIME HORIZON'

'Fair enough. Let's look at the third component then: what's the time horizon? When will your goal be achieved?'

'Now you're really asking me to be a prophet!' said Howard.

'Let me help you. Typically, visions should be achievable within three to five years. Some experts suggest an even longer period. Setting a goal that far into the future requires thinking beyond your current capabilities and current environment. It forces you and your team to be visionary, rather than just tactical. I like business guru Jim Collins' rule of thumb that a 50 to 70 per cent probability of success is enough.'

Howard thought about it for a few moments. 'Achieving that goal in five years is a big ask, but I believe it's possible.'

'Good. Then once you've designed the strategies to back it up – which we'll focus on shortly – it should be a compelling vision for your staff and for the buyers of your business.'

DIFFERENTIATION

'So now that I have an inspiring vision, how do I go about achieving it?' asked Howard.

'Ah, that's the million-dollar question.'

'If we're servicing 600 of the top UK law firms and 500 leading UK accountants and banks in five years, it will be a lot more than just a one-million dollar question,' said Howard with a laugh.

'To achieve your vision, you'll need to influence your target market to engage with you and your products. And that requires you to differentiate VinciWorks in the minds of your prospects and customers, relative to the competition.'

'How do I do that?' Howard asked.

'First, you need to understand what drives your customers to buy. This means deeply understanding their needs – both in relation to your products or services *and* the whole purchase experience. For instance, if you're buying a car, you might be influenced by the car's features. Is it spacious, luxurious, fast, economical? But you may also be influenced by the purchase experience: how friendly, helpful, knowledgeable and trustworthy is the salesperson? How easy and straightforward is the payment process?

'If you don't deeply understand these needs, it's unlikely you'll be able to craft marketing collateral, advertising copy or sales pitches that speak to your customers' needs. For example, if your target market is hard on cash and looking for a low-cost product but you focus on how environmentally friendly your solution is, you'll miss the mark. And if you don't know what your customers really need and care about, you won't be able to design products and services that target those needs in ways that differentiate you from the competition.'

'But isn't it obvious that a business must offer products or services that meet people's needs?'

'Perhaps,' said Joel. 'But you'd be surprised how many businesses struggle to do so in ways that truly differentiate them.

Which leads me to question whether they truly get it. Let me ask you: do you know what truly drives your customers to buy your products?'

'I'm in the online training business, so for me it's easy. My clients buy my products because they need to train their staff.'

'Hang on a second. Training is the end product; it's the solution to their need. But it's not the underlying need they're trying to satisfy. Why do your clients need to train their staff in the first place?'

'You mean aside from the fact that, in the industries we serve, it's a mandatory, regulated requirement?'

'Meeting mandatory requirements is an important need. But when it really comes down to it, what's the pain they're trying to relieve, what desire are they trying to satisfy or what goals are they trying to achieve or protect?'

'I guess they're ultimately trying to keep their staff out of prison, avoid fines and protect the reputation of their firms.'

'Now we're talking. Tell me more about what you mean by that.'

Howard sat back and organised his thoughts before speaking.

'We produce anti-money laundering training, for example. The law requires employees working in businesses that deal with money, like banks, law firms and accounting practices, to report to the authorities any client they suspect may be involved in laundering money. In many countries, such as the UK, it's a criminal offence if a member of staff was or should have been suspicious and yet failed to make a report. If found guilty, the staff member *and* the responsible partners or senior managers can go to prison for up to 14 years. So we train everyone in the firm to recognise suspicious activities and know when and how to report them.'

'Staying out of prison is a pretty serious need!' said Joel.

Joel continued to drill down into the driving needs of Howard's customers. Howard produced a full list of needs and circled the most critical, urgent ones.

'Okay, now we need to identify which of those needs you'll meet better than anyone else. That's what will truly differentiate you.'

'And why exactly do I need to do that?' asked Howard.

'Think of it this way: a business that exists without a key differentiator is sending the message: *Buy from me for no particular reason.*'

Howard couldn't resist a smile. 'Yes, I guess that's not a very powerful message.'

'Right, which is why you need to clearly answer the question all potential customers ask, at least subconsciously: "Why should I buy from VinciWorks instead of any other supplier?"'

'Good question!'

'Yes. A question you need to ask yourself. The answer is sometimes called your Unique Selling Proposition or your Competitive Advantage. It actually doesn't matter what you call it, so long as you can make a legitimate claim to being better in some respect. It could be related to your service, your pricing, your selection, the convenience, speed of delivery, your warranties, the exclusivity of your offerings, how socially conscious you are, how much fun people have dealing with you, how cool or hip your image is, and so on.'

Howard responded quickly. 'I can confidently say that we offer extremely high-value products with great service. We're not the cheapest, but we're very fair.'

'Those are good qualities, but how do they differentiate you? Everyone expects quality products, great customer service and to be dealt with fairly and honestly. They are threshold requirements that are necessary just to keep you in the game and prevent you from going out of business. None of those qualities makes you unique or different.

'The question you need to answer is: what's your unique value to your market? If you can answer that question in a clear, compelling and verifiable way, you can differentiate VinciWorks and you're in with a chance of achieving your stretch goals. If not, you'll just be another provider fighting for market share and survival.'

'I've never thought of my business like this before. That's scary.'

'You're right. Very few small businesses go through this process deliberately. It's one of the reasons that very few achieve the success they desire.'

Howard took a deep breath. 'Look, I can make loads of claims about being better, stronger, faster, more experienced, more accurate and more current. And in my own mind and in my heart, I know they're true. But to truly differentiate I can see that I need to prove it.'

'That's right. And you could do so with client testimonials, unique qualifications and case studies. Or you could link your offer to a guarantee that puts your money where your mouth is – and therefore builds legitimacy.'

'Yes, but anyone can get friendly clients to create fantastical testimonials. Can you give me some examples of compelling differentiators?'

'Examples of specific, measurable differentiators could include things like: "My system gives you all the power of the leading three brands but for thousands of pounds less and here's a pricing and features comparison table." Or the famous Domino's Pizza guarantee: "Fresh, hot pizza, delivered in less than 30 minutes or it's free." Or: "The only restaurant where you can get your car washed and your clothes dry-cleaned while you eat great food." Or: "If we can't sell your house in three months, we'll buy it – at our listing price!"'

Howard thought again. 'I don't have differentiators like the examples you gave but I think my core business model is a unique differentiator.'

'What do you mean?' asked Joel.

'Well, it's the way we develop our compliance training. We call it Collaborative Development. It's based on the principle that "there is no competitive advantage in compliance". We bring together competitive companies to collaboratively develop solutions and, by so doing, we instantly establish industry best practice. By collaborating with their peers, our clients are able to share resources and expertise with the best companies in their industry, build better solutions and do so at lower cost per firm.'

'That is unique,' said Joel. 'How did you pull that together?'

'When the money laundering regulations came into force, I was asked by one of the largest global law firms to build them an online training course. I said, "Sure, I'd love to. Just send me the content." But they didn't have any content, the regulations were very broad and they didn't know what training to provide, who to train, how much or how regularly to train. So I initially contacted four other leading firms and asked what they were doing to solve the problem. I guess, in your language, Joel, I was discovering a driving need. It immediately became clear that they all had the same problem but no one had a clear solution. So I proposed that I would facilitate them working together to collaboratively create the training.

'It began with a group of 14 law firms, including nine of the top ten in the UK. Between them, the group employed almost 30 per cent of all UK lawyers, so together they instantly established best practice for the profession as a whole. By collaborating with their peers they were all better protected. If one of the firms messed up and ended up facilitating a money-laundering scheme, the judge, when sentencing, would be likely to ask if the firm had fulfilled its regulatory duty to provide training and if the training was "good enough". By collaborating, they create "safety in numbers". Each firm could say: "I don't know what 'good enough' means but we provide the same high quality training as all other major firms in the profession." And we are the only company able to offer firms that level of assurance. Also, because our clients help us build the products that they then buy, we have a guaranteed market while they get better training at a lot lower cost per firm. It's a true win–win solution.'

'And, as well as being an exceptional differentiator, it's a great barrier to competitive entry,' said Joel. 'Howard, this means you can genuinely say that you meet the needs of "keeping people out of jail and protecting company reputations" better than any others because you're leveraging the collective wisdom of the top law firms in the world.'

'You know, Joel, I didn't really appreciate how good a model it is until right now.'

'Okay,' said Joel. 'Let's capture this idea in a pithy, memorable statement, often called your Brand Promise. You want a phrase that summarises the compelling promise you're making to your target market. It can also become the basis for your slogan or tag line.'

More excited about the process and the business than he had been in years, Howard proposed, '"Leveraging industry expertise and reducing costs through collaborative development." Or maybe: "Establishing industry standards and reducing costs through collaborative development."'

'They both have potential; just be sure to be as succinct as possible,' said Joel. 'How about you work on it as part of your homework. It may take some time to nail it.'

Joel and Howard took a short break but decided to press on through the afternoon to see if they could complete a first draft by the end of the day. It was intense but Howard was surprised at how quickly and painlessly Joel had led him through the process.

During the afternoon, Joel encouraged Howard to identify a number of Strategic Objectives (or key areas of focus) for the business over the next five years in order to achieve his big-picture vision, including:

- Growing sales by extending the collaborative development model into the financial and accounting services sectors;
- Improving VinciWorks' product offerings by developing and promoting their risk-management software; and
- Getting internal operations systematised and working smoothly so the business didn't depend on Howard's constant involvement – in particular, its financial management.

Having completed the Strategic Direction phase of the Business Plan, Joel helped Howard work through the Strategic Execution components. They began by defining tangible success measures for each strategic objective, so that the goals were crystal clear. By the time they finished, Howard had a clear target for VinciWorks to grow annual revenues from £1,000,000 to £10,000,000 by 2020.

To help Howard achieve these goals, Joel took him through a SWOT analysis. 'A SWOT analysis – SWOT being an acronym for Strengths, Weaknesses, Opportunities and Threats,' explained Joel, 'helps you bring into focus all the critical factors affecting your business, and lays the foundation for intelligent decision-making about how you'll bridge the gap between where you are now and where you want to be.'

Together they examined the current state of the business, including its internal strengths and weaknesses, as well as the opportunities and threats in its external environment. Joel drew four equal quadrants (Strengths, Weaknesses, Opportunities and Threats) on the whiteboard and asked Howard to begin filling in the boxes. Together they compiled a long list and then highlighted what Howard felt were the most significant items in each category.

- **Strengths:** collaborative development process establishes key barrier to entry for competitors.
- **Opportunities:** ever-increasing need for compliance in other professional services sectors, just like in the legal sector.
- **Weaknesses:** lack of systems, especially around financial management.
- **Threats:** SRA (Solicitors Regulatory Authority) potentially changing the playing field by making CPD points (Continuing Professional Development) no longer mandatory; and the Law Society going into direct competition with VinciWorks.

Finally, informed by the SWOT analysis, they identified a number of strategic projects to focus on for the current year, and they mapped out detailed 90-day action plans for the projects designated for the upcoming quarter. Joel explained that if Howard were to implement the plan, he'd recommend instituting quarterly reviews to check progress and create action plans for the next 90 days.

Over the next week, Howard reviewed and refined the business plan further. As he presented his final version to Joel in their next meeting, he was overcome with a bittersweet feeling. 'You know, Joel, I'm so thankful for your help. Before we began I didn't appreciate the problems the business faced. But even more importantly, I was blind to what the business could be. I was trying to hit a bullseye without actually having a target.

'Now I'm genuinely sad at the thought of selling. I now understand why the buyers might be willing to pay the price they've offered. I truly believe in the plan and, although it's ambitious, I can see how the business could be generating £10 million by 2020. On the other hand, based on where things sit today, the current offer is generous and just about enough to make me sell.'

Joel stared at Howard for an uncomfortably long time. 'Howard, we've created a compelling plan, but don't forget the stress, pressure and struggle that the business currently represents. I believe you could do it, but it would still be a long journey to take the business from where it is today to £10 million or more in profitable revenue.'

'I know,' replied Howard. 'But how many times in life do you get to go on that type of journey?'

SUMMARY

BUSINESS PLANNING

» There are two fundamental components to an effective business plan:

- A clear sense of where you're going (Strategic Direction); and
- A well-considered plan for how to get there (Strategic Execution).

» If either one is missing, your chances of success diminish.

» Your Strategic Direction and your Strategic Execution can be broken down into ten critical components.

Strategic Direction

PURPOSE — Why do we exist? What kind of impact to we want to have?

VALUES — What attitudes or behaviours are critical to achieving our purpose?

VISION — What will the future look like if we're successfully fulfilling our purpose?

DIFFERENTIATION — What factors will distinguish us from others and underpin our unique brand promise?

STRATEGIC OBJECTIVES — What areas will we need to focus on to achieve our Vision?

Strategic Execution

SUCCESS MEASURES — How will we measure our performance in 3-5 yrs & 1 yr?

CURRENT REALITY — What are our current strengths, weaknesses, opportunities & threats?

STRATEGIC PROJECTS — What will we do this yr to hit our 1yr targets?

ACTION PLAN — What specific actions are needed this Qtr?

PROGRESS REVIEW — How will we monitor progress?

LEANING IN

The 22nd of December 2013 was a burning summer's day in Melbourne. At 40 degrees Celsius, the wind blew hot, and bushfires tore through the brittle undergrowth of the Victorian countryside. Eucalyptus trees exploded into searing fireballs that devoured the trees, homes and people in their path. The smoke billowed so high and wide that it could be seen from the suburbs.

When Howard opened the curtains of his bedroom window, the scene outside looked ominous. Dark thoughts filled his mind. Was this foreshadowing the fate of his business? There had been no response to the extensive business plan he'd submitted, and the agreed deadline for the sale was only two days away.

After successfully solving a potential issue over intellectual property, everything had gone quiet. Nigel had gone quiet too. Howard's advisors told him not to panic, that everything slows down before the holidays. But Howard's instinct told him that something was not right. Andrea was keen to talk about the family holiday they had agreed to take – the first in years – as soon as the money arrived, but Howard was nervous to discuss a future that was starting to feel uncertain.

Finally, after two days of chasing, an email from Howard's legal advisor arrived on Christmas Eve. The buyers were not willing to proceed on the agreed terms. Instead, they presented a revised offer that cut the original offer by more than 50 per cent and converted a substantial amount of the cash payment into an earn-out. Howard had demanded 'an unreasonable offer' – unreasonably good, that is. The new offer was now worse than 'reasonable'. They were trying to buy the business at a fire-sale value.

'What the hell is going on? What are they thinking?' screamed Howard to Nigel over the crackling Skype line.

'I have no idea. This is first I've heard of it. I know this reduced offer has come as a shock but given the sales figures over the last six to 12 months, it's not so bad. It's still a "reasonable offer". It's just that the bulk of the payment is an earn-out.'

'The earn-out is ridiculous. I only get paid if the business achieves the forecasts,' said Howard.

'Well, aren't you confident of the forecasts? They were in your business plan.'

'Yes, I am confident of the numbers. But one of their conditions – or should I say one of *your* conditions – is that I'm not involved in managing the business during the period of the earn-out. Even if I thought you could deliver the revenues, they or you could easily orchestrate it to keep the numbers just below the target. And unless you hit the target, I get nothing, zero, not even a proportion.'

And then it all became clear – like an epiphany – and Nigel's entire plan unfurled in Howard's mind. *Nigel's right. The offer is so low because sales over the last year were among the worst in the company's history, the exact period in which Nigel was in control. And now the buyers are insistent that I'm out and Nigel run the show. It feels like a set-up.*

'We've signed a Heads of Agreement, we had a deal,' said Howard, pulling himself out of his thoughts. 'Andrea has planned a family trip, the kids are so excited about me being home and not travelling every five minutes. I don't know how I'll break it to them if it all falls through.'

'Yes, I know. And even if you do say no we are still in a tough position.'

'I'm fully aware of the situation. If I say no I'm going to have to pick things up, take back control of the business and try to make things right.'

'But we already know that running the business remotely from Australia doesn't work,' said Nigel. 'I'm happy to carry on, but I can't guarantee to fix things. It's tough out there right now. It's been tough for a while.'

'You're right. If I say no I'll have to commit to spending all or most of my time in London – at least until things turn around, or until I fail.'

'Howard, come on, be honest with yourself. There's no way you're going to leave Australia, leave Andrea and your kids, your friends, your community. And as you said, you can't pull your girls out of high school with exams coming up. That would go against all your principles. I know you better than that.'

'The whole thing stinks,' said Howard, sitting with Andrea at the kitchen table. As usual, his wife amazed him, seemingly taking the news in her stride and hugging him with a reassurance that he so desperately needed.

'Nigel doesn't know you. He doesn't know you like I know you. It's another set-up. He has run the business into the ground and now intends to effectively steal it from you. I bet he planned this from the beginning, from the time he ambushed you and convinced you to step back. Don't you think it's a coincidence that just when you were ready to regain control and fire him, he comes up with these buyers who were going to pay you a stupid amount of money, way more than what the business is worth?'

'Not *way* more,' said Howard. 'It's a good business with great potential. I proved that in the business plan.'

'Then get off your arse and go to London and prove it in the real world! You told me that deep down you're sad about selling the business before you could turn it into the success you believe it can be. Well, go and make it happen. Nigel is relying on you feeling so guilty about spending even more time away from us that you'll take the low-ball offer. And then he'll only just fail to reach the earn-out target. But Nigel doesn't know you and he doesn't know us. We love you and we trust you. Speak to the kids and ask them. You need to go for yourself and for us. As much as I don't want you to go, the money from the sale won't last long and we will be back in the same financial situation but with nowhere to go. You're an entrepreneur, a loving and caring entrepreneur, but still an entrepreneur. If you don't go, you'll go nuts and you'll drive us nuts. At the very least, think about it, speak with Joel and speak with Aryeh. We are here, we will be here whenever you come home, whether it's once a month or once every six months. Go and make it a success, so that one day I can have that dream Porsche,' said Andrea with a cheeky smile.

In his gut Howard knew that Andrea was right. He really did hate leaving the family, but maybe it was time to rise to the challenge. He called Aryeh and they arranged to meet that evening.

REFLECTION

'I know that if I reject the offer and step back in as CEO, I'll need to be in the UK more than I'm at home and there's no guarantee that I'll do any better than in the past,' moaned Howard. 'In fact, the odds are that I'll just repeat the same mistakes.'

'Yes, being away from the family will be hard,' said Aryeh. 'Let's talk about how to handle that as a separate issue. But in relation to the business, why don't you ask Joel to advise you on how to run it more effectively and set it up to run without you needing to be there all the time? Isn't that what he helps business owners do?'

'I intend to get his help with the business. I'm just concerned that the issue is also with me, personally. I remember what you said about reality-testing my failure story. I've been practising that. And it's helped me. But when I try to think about the situation in terms of how I can grow and learn from it, I'm not even sure where to start. I don't know what I need to learn to avoid making the same mistakes.'

'Sometimes our mistakes are obvious and what we need to learn is clear. All we need is a growth mindset and we're off. But you're right; in some situations it's not so obvious. In these cases, I recommend a process of self-reflection. I do it every time I make a mistake. In fact, I do it every day. It's what the mystics call *Teshuva*.'

'*Teshuva*?'

'It's a term for a very practical method of self-reflection.'

'Okay, tell me more.'

'Well, it's not particularly complicated. There are three steps: (1) Introspection; (2) Articulation; and (3) Commitment. I'll walk you through each one.'

1: INTROSPECTION

'You start with introspection,' said Aryeh. 'It's a process of identifying and becoming aware of your mistakes.'

'And how exactly do I do that?'

'You need to step out of your current situation and look at it objectively. I find it helpful to begin by minimising external distractions. Turn off your phone, go to a space where you can think clearly. Perhaps go for a drive or a walk to clear your mind and create the space for introspective thinking.'

'Joel says that I need to stop working *in* my business and start working *on* my business by looking at it objectively as if it were separate from me. Are you saying that I need to do something similar here?'

'Yes, in a sense you could say that.'

'Is this a process of beating myself up? I'm pretty good at that already!'

'No, this is not about developing guilt. It's about deeply understanding that we are all susceptible to error. The real breakthrough for many people is recognising that those errors can act as the motivation for transformational change and movement towards your purpose.

'We've all heard of the man who, for 20 years, was told by doctors that if he continued his existing lifestyle, his life expectancy was limited. Then he had a massive heart attack but miraculously survived. Within weeks he became one of the fittest and healthiest men around.'

'Yes, I know several people like that. So must we all have heart attacks to learn our lesson?'

'Not always. If he had listened to the doctors, he may not

have needed a near-death experience to wake him up. But sometimes we do need a jolt to help us confront the issues we don't yet recognise.'

'What you're saying is to think about what went wrong and consider how I've contributed to it.'

'Simply put, yes. But here's a process that makes it much easier, especially if this is the first time you're doing it.

'First, focus on a past unsuccessful experience. Try to recall your thoughts, emotions and behaviour at that time. Then identify the outcome you wanted to achieve and diagnose why you were unable to achieve that outcome. I find it helpful to come up with at least ten answers to the question: "I didn't achieve this outcome because …"'

'Ten sounds like a lot,' said Howard.

'It is and it's deliberate. It forces you to dig deep, beyond the superficial explanations. But don't worry, once you have your ten, you select the three answers you consider most significant. And for each one, you ask yourself: "What can I learn about myself from this answer?" Be on the lookout for unhelpful thought patterns, habits or stories you were telling yourself. If these themes are playing out in multiple situations, you may well be onto something important.'

'That's intense. If all of that is step one, I'm not sure I want to know about step two.'

2: ARTICULATION

'Step two is simple,' said Aryeh. 'It's called articulation. It's about verbalising how we've contributed to the situation. There's something very powerful about verbalising our contribution, either orally or in writing. It helps you separate yourself from what you did or didn't do, enabling you to achieve some level of objectivity and helping you deal with it rationally. You don't need to communicate this to anyone else, but I find that writing it down in a personal journal is very helpful. It enables me to review it to assess my progress and help me deal with similar challenges in the future.'

'So this isn't a one-time fix or instant cure then? My issues are going to come back and haunt me forever?'

'That depends to some extent on how sincerely you work through this process and how honest you are with yourself. If you just skim over an issue and don't deal with it properly, it might well reoccur. And yes, some issues do require significant internal work that can't be resolved in single sitting.'

3: COMMITMENT

'The last step is the most important,' said Aryeh. 'It's where you commit to moving forward. Once you've identified what's holding you back, you need to consciously let go of those things and decide what you're going to do differently in the future.'

'Okay, I think I get it,' said Howard, not entirely sure whether in fact he did get it.

'You should know that all I'm giving you here are the tools. You'll need to apply them yourself. It's a very personal process. Give it a go and keep me posted on your progress.'

The next day, Howard decided to engage in some self-reflection. He got into his car, dropped the convertible roof and drove down the Great Ocean Road, doing his best to think about where it all went wrong and how he got into his current situation. He followed a nondescript country road heading nowhere in particular − at least nowhere he'd been before. He soon found himself completely alone, parked on a slight crest with a perfect view of the sparkling, greenish-blue ocean.

Choosing a past unsuccessful situation was the easy part. He could think of many. But the one that stood out in his mind was the cash-flow crisis he'd faced a few months back. He called that experience to mind − the 3.00 a.m. wakings, the stress, the dark thoughts, the impact on his family. It was all too vivid.

In that situation, his desired outcome was a healthy stream of cash in the business. He then tried Aryeh's formula to diagnose why it hadn't turned out that way. *Why didn't I achieve that outcome?* he asked himself. *I didn't achieve this outcome because … the market was tough. We'd barely emerged from the global financial crisis; law firms were cutting costs left, right and centre. Nigel should have been more proactive in seeking new clients, rather than staying in his comfort zone and servicing existing ones. And getting prompt payment from clients themselves is like pulling teeth.*

Howard counted his answers and realised he'd only come up with three and needed at least ten. He also realised that none of the answers related to him and his contribution. *I suppose the fact that clients didn't pay on time wasn't only their fault. We proved that with the collections system. If I'd been on top of our collections process, we would have been in a much better position,* he conceded.

And as much as I hate to admit it, if I had been on top of Nigel, I would have known he wasn't meeting new clients. I could have given him that feedback much earlier, even though he's experienced enough to have known that without my feedback.

Howard came up with ten explanations, many of which related to the way he managed the business. *What can I learn about myself from these explanations?* he asked himself. *Is there a theme running through them?* And that's when it hit him. He'd abdicated responsibility. He was the owner *of* the business, but he hadn't taken 'ownership' *for* the business. He knew that micromanagement wasn't the answer, but he also realised that relying on others and then blaming them without giving clear direction, vision and systems to empower them to do their jobs was *his* issue.

He began grieving for the loss and the opportunities he hadn't fulfilled. And he even said it out loud to himself. He then reflected again on the business plan. *The opportunity is still there, if only I can begin taking ownership. I've caused pain to my family. I'm now going to have to go away to do it right and set it up properly. The business can run without me, but only if I create it that way. I can't just sit back and hope that it will run itself. I need to have the courage to make it happen, the confidence to do it the way I think it should be done. I am fortunate to have some amazing advisors, but ultimately it's up to me. NO EXCUSES!*

Taking a deep breath, he began the drive home. He was feeling drained but also excited. A weight had been lifted and some clarity had emerged. At some level, he felt deeply grateful that the opportunity to achieve his vision was still available.

He drove straight to the office and called his co-directors, followed by Nigel and the buyers. He told them the deal was off. The conviction in his voice made it clear that there was no point arguing. The buyers and Nigel were both angry and surprised. They thought they had him cornered.

He then called Joel to set up a meeting for the following day, as well as Aryeh to share his reflection, insights and resulting decision.

Howard put the phone down, sat back and said to himself, 'Create the greatest sustainable value. No Excuses!' Now was the time, his time, his opportunity. No more excuses.

SUMMARY

REFLECTION

In situations where our mistakes – and what we can learn from them – aren't obvious, our ability to learn, grow and succeed depends on engaging in a process of honest self-reflection.

There are three key steps:

(1) Introspection – to identify and become aware of your contribution to the situation, find a quiet, conducive environment and then:

- Focus on a past unsuccessful experience.
- Call that experience to mind – try to recall your thoughts, emotions and behaviour.

- Identify the outcome you wanted to achieve in that situation.
- Diagnose why you were unable to achieve that outcome by coming up with at least ten answers to the question: 'I didn't achieve this outcome because ...'
- Select the top three most significant explanations, and for each of them ask yourself: 'What can I learn about myself from this explanation?' Consider any unhelpful thought patterns or stories you're telling, as well as personality traits or habits you've adopted. Look out for 'themes' that may be playing out in other situations, too.

(2) Articulation – articulate how you've contributed to the situation, either in writing or orally.

(3) Commitment – commit to what you're going to do differently in the future.

FREE RESOURCES: To download concise summaries, templates and resources to help you apply the principles in this chapter, go to www.mindfulentrepreneur.co/resources

GOING INTO TRAINING

The sun was already shining through the blinds when Howard arrived at his office, later than usual. He'd decided to drive his youngest daughter to school, instead of her taking the bus, and have breakfast with her on the way. Despite having made a definitive decision to rebuild VinciWorks, he was equally determined to maintain focus on his family. He loved spending quality, one-on-one time with each of his daughters, and he refused to give that up.

Over a coffee with Joel, Howard shared his insights about taking ownership and responsibility.

'Now it's not just theory. We wrote a business plan and I need your help to execute it,' explained Howard.

'I'd be delighted to help you. Though I should warn you that we'll have a lot of work to do and it won't necessarily be comfortable or easy.'

'I've made my decision and there is no turning back now, so where do we start?'

'We identified a few strategic objectives in your business plan. The two most critical seemed to be: growing sales and getting your internal operations working smoothly, without your constant involvement. I understand the urgency of growing sales, but I'm concerned that if we don't get your internal operations in order first, you won't be able to deliver effectively even if you do grow – not to mention the impact of the increased work on your sanity and personal life.

'So I suggest we begin with systematising and stabilising the internal operations. With a properly structured and well-managed base, we can quickly turn our focus to growing sales. How does that sound?'

'That sounds right. As you proved with the collections process and as we learned through writing the business plan, we virtually have no systems to speak of. Let's say it how it is: right now it's a mess and I am afraid that if I don't get the house in order, the life-blood of the business – our renewal revenues – will be at risk. So I guess we start with systems then?'

'We'll certainly need systems,' said Joel. 'But it's more than just systems. We need to introduce four kinds of clarity in your business: (1) structural clarity, so everyone is clear on what jobs need to get done and who's responsible for each job; (2) job clarity, so the expectations in each job are clear; (3) task clarity, so everyone knows how to perform the key tasks within each job – that's where systems come in; and (4) performance clarity, so you know whether you're achieving the intended results.'

'Okay, you're the boss.'

'No,' said Joel, 'you decided on the Great Ocean Road that *you're* going to be the boss. I'm merely going to help you become a better boss. And with that in mind, let's create some structural clarity by defining exactly who's responsible for the various jobs and tasks in your business. That's your first job if you want to establish yourself as a true leader.'

ORGANISATIONAL STRUCTURE

'I'll start with a simple question,' continued Joel. 'Think about it carefully before you answer, though. Are your staff clear about who's responsible for each task in your business?'

'Before we began working together, I would probably have said yes. Most tasks end up getting done so presumably people must know what they need to do. But if our previous collections process is anything to go by, it's obvious that there's confusion about who's doing what. We learned that my bookkeeper, for example, clearly didn't agree with what I assumed was her responsibility while others got involved in the process but for the wrong reasons.'

'Okay, so you can clearly see the problem. Do you have a feel for how widely or deeply the problem runs?'

'I'm not sure, to be honest. And I don't know how I'd find out, either. I know I said I want to take ownership, but I don't want to start looking over the shoulder of every staff member and watching their every move. I don't believe in micromanagement. I've always tried to respect my staff and give them the space to work.'

'And that's a good thing. Autonomy is important; micromanaging is unproductive and de-motivating. But it's still critical that everyone's clear on exactly which jobs they're responsible for *before* you empower them to assume that responsibility.'

'I guess I can accept that. I can see that that is the difference between abdicating responsibility and taking responsibility. That's exactly what I need to work on.'

'That's right,' said Joel, gratified that Howard had come to this realisation on his own. 'The fact is you won't be able grow your business alone. You need people. That's obvious. But what's not always obvious to time-poor leaders is that *people need organisation*. To empower your people to deliver the results you want, your first step is to create an organisational structure that clarifies exactly which jobs need to get done, who's responsible for doing them and who reports to whom. And an effective way to do this is to create an organisational chart.'

'Yeah, we have something like that. I'm CEO, Josh is finance and operations, Nigel is head of sales and Natalie does the bookkeeping and manages customer service.'

'Okay, that's a start. But it only goes part of the way. Let me explain by dispelling a myth: the primary purpose of your organisational chart is *not* to map out the people you happen to employ in your business. It does that too, but there's more to it.'

Joel stopped and took a sip of his coffee before continuing. He knew his next point was pivotal to Howard's success, but he also knew that it represented a paradigm-shift for business owners and was sometimes difficult to grasp.

'If you're at all familiar with the building process, you'll know that once the architect has created the detailed, visionary blueprint of the building, it's time to hand the plans to a structural design engineer to map out the internal structure – including which beams and posts need to go where to support the intended function of the building.

'It's the same with any business: you need to create a structural design of the key jobs and tasks that must take place in each area of the business to support your vision. Once you have that infra-structure in place, you can *then* decide *who* should fill each job in that structure.'

'I'm not sure I get it.'

'Okay, have you ever thrown people into jobs you know they're not really suited to?' asked Joel.

Howard thought for a moment. 'Yes, I have, if they were the only ones willing or available to do the job. But what choice did I have? In a small business, people need to step up to the plate and do whatever they're called on to do.'

'You need staff who can be nimble and flexible from time to time. And that's okay, *if* they have the capacity to do the job properly. But keeping someone in a job they're not able to perform effectively doesn't help you. Does that make sense?'

'I suppose so. When I think about it, I'm probably also guilty of allowing staff to do jobs they're good at and want to do, rather than the jobs the business actually needs them to do.'

'Exactly. That's what happens when you fit jobs around people rather than people around jobs. When you define the jobs that must be performed by the business to achieve success *before* allocating specific people to those jobs, something powerful happens: you're able to objectively assess whether the *right* jobs are getting done in the *right* way to achieve your vision. And depending on your answer, you can then work out who are the *right* people for those jobs.'

Howard considered what Joel said.

'Just one more point that's particularly relevant to you,' continued Joel. 'Your organisational chart serves another purpose. It will help you achieve one of your key personal goals. As you chart the various jobs in your business, you'll almost certainly find that *you* are occupying a number of different jobs.

'This realisation is critical because once you identify the various jobs you're responsible for (or interfere in), you can make deliberate, strategic decisions about which jobs you *should* be doing, which jobs you *want* to do (if any), and which jobs you should *delegate* to others.'

'So once I reorganise I can just chill out and let everyone else do the work?' Howard said.

'Eventually, maybe. For now, you'll probably still need to fill multiple jobs. But you'll be able to plan for an organisational structure that aligns with your personal goals – whether that's to focus only on the parts of your business you enjoy or even to pull away from the business altogether. It will be your choice.'

'I get it. Where do I start?'

'At its most basic level, an organisational chart is a hierarchical grouping of boxes (representing key functions or jobs) linked by lines (showing reporting relationships), with job titles in each box. To create an accurate chart, there are a few key steps. You start by recording the name of every key task that must get done to run and grow the business. Then you group those tasks into coherent, defined jobs. This stage often reveals the dysfunction in your current structure; many businesses have related tasks being handled by completely random people – often simply because it happened to be that way historically. Next, you need to decide who's responsible for each job. Finally, you consider which jobs need to be filled or changed to help realise your vision.'

'There are literally dozens of tasks that need to get done,' said Howard. 'I wouldn't even know where to start. How am I supposed to write them all down?'

'It helps to start by breaking your business down into its five core task areas.' Joel drew a basic diagram on the whiteboard depicting these five areas.

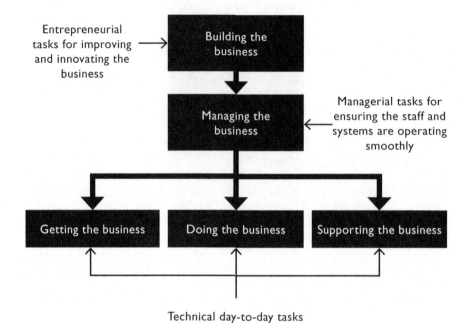

'In fact, we could break those areas down even further.' Joel expanded his diagram on the whiteboard.

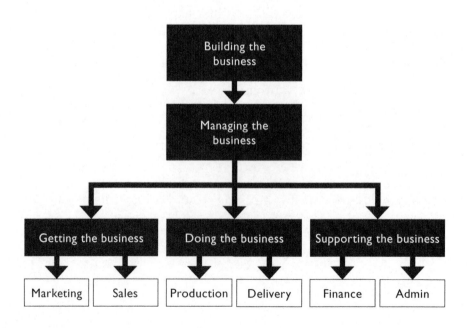

'Let's start with "Getting the business". Within that area, you have two sub-task areas: sales and marketing. Start with one of them – let's take your sales function, for example. What sales tasks happen or need to happen to convert potential customers into actual customers?'

Howard took a deep breath, fearing the extent of the effort. But once he began, it flowed quite quickly. He knew his business and what it took to sell and deliver his products.

'Well, there's …

- Handling customer queries
- Cold/warm calling/emailing
- Scheduling appointments
- Conducting a needs analysis
- Delivering a sales pitch
- Preparing estimates/quotes
- Negotiating terms
- Sending forms and contracts for signing.'

'Perfect,' said Joel. 'Now do that for each area. Just use some lined pages and create task lists under each area, or fire up an Excel spreadsheet if you prefer. I'm going to make a phone call. Let me know when you're finished.'

Almost an hour later, Howard completed his first cut and showed it to Joel.

Joel made some minor changes, but was impressed by Howard's

first attempt. 'Now it's time to group the tasks into categories that represent actual, coherent jobs.'

'How do I know which tasks fall into which jobs?'

'My rule of thumb is this: if they relate to a similar skillset and they could all be done by one person, it's a single job. For example, you've listed a range of marketing-related tasks – creating news-letters, making flyers, social media postings, and so on. It would make sense to group them under a single job, like marketing coor-dinator, for instance. The only exception is if there's a good reason for specialising certain tasks to create efficiencies. For example, a warehouse operations job could be split into a picking job, a packing job and an inventory control job.'

Howard looked at his long task list. 'I think I know what you mean. I have multiple customer support tasks in my list. To operate those tasks I currently have one person doing customer implementations, another doing training and responding to customer inquiries and a third person doing general and technical customer support. But I should really merge the implementation and training tasks into one job because they're quite similar and connected skillsets.

'On the other hand, I should probably separate the general customer support and technical support tasks into two different job roles – technical issues require specialised IT expertise and are very different to general support questions.'

'Excellent! I can see you really get it.'

'It isn't rocket science, is it? In fact, it's a bit embarrassing recognising just how much of a mess and how inefficient my structure actually is.'

'Don't be embarrassed. This is precisely the value of stepping back and working *on* your business instead of *in* it.'

'Forest from the trees,' said Howard.

'Exactly. Now have a go at grouping the rest of your tasks into jobs.'

Howard began working out loud. 'Looking at my sales tasks, I think there should be two jobs: a sales rep job to do cold-calling, meet prospects and customers, carry out client needs analyses, make sales pitches and close deals; and a sales support job to qualify prospects, schedule appointments, create written proposals and quotes, and then send terms and conditions and contracts once the deal has been closed. Does that sound right?'

'You know your business best, but yes, it sounds very reasonable.'

Howard took some time to group all the tasks into jobs and presented it to Joel.

'Okay, good work, almost done. Now just give each job an appropriate title and allocate your people to those jobs. Here's what I'd suggest: take out a pencil and a large blank piece of paper, draw the jobs as boxes with job titles and connect them with reporting lines. Then write your name and the names of your staff into the appropriate boxes.'

A short while later, Howard completed the task. 'I thought my business was relatively simple, but there really are so many tasks that need to get done. And I'm a little shocked – although I probably shouldn't be – at how many tasks *I'm* doing. I'd love to pass some of these over, but I just don't know if my people can handle them. I get annoyed when people don't do things to the standards I expect and, given how badly Nigel managed the business over the last few months, I have little trust, to be honest.'

'To use your words, Howard, those issues can be handled by taking genuine *ownership*, rather than *abdicating* responsibility. And that's not about micromanagement; it's about creating job descriptions and systems and proper accountability mechanisms. But for the moment, don't worry too much about how you'll actually pass over the jobs; just identify which ones you'd *like* to pass over.'

Howard looked back at the organisational chart that now filled the page. 'I'm essentially managing the finances. I'm looking at the bank account every day to check that we have enough cash. I'd love to pass that over. I'm also writing the copy for our marketing materials and reviewing the content for our courses. I don't really need to be doing either of those tasks. In truth, it looks like I have my hand in almost everything! No wonder I'm cream-crackered!'

'Cream-crackered?'

'Cream-crackered – you know, knackered … exhausted. Don't worry, it's just Cockney rhyming slang. Whistle and flute – suit; pots and lids – kids; trouble and strife – wife.'

Joel smiled. 'Cream-crackered or not, recognising your involvement in so many tasks is an important insight, particularly when you can also see that you're not necessarily the best person to do them all. And even more so if you want to set up the business so you can spend more quality time with your family.'

'There's one last step. Look back at your chart and ask yourself:

- Is everyone being utilised appropriately? Could anyone take on more work, for example?
- Is anyone being spread too thinly? Should work be taken away from them – or their hours increased?
- Is anyone in a job for which they're not suited?'

Howard studied the chart carefully, while Joel wrote up the questions on the whiteboard.

'The answer is probably yes to all of those questions. But until we broke it down into this chart, I had no idea which people and which tasks. It's pretty clear to me that if I'm going to be in London doing the sales rep/business development job, I really don't need Nigel.'

'What would that mean to you and the business?' asked Joel.

'Well, first and foremost, it would save us £150,000 a year in salary and benefits that could go to employing people who could manage a number of tasks that are simply not being handled right now. There are lots of marketing tasks that are either not getting done or are being done in a haphazard, ineffective way by the wrong people.

'If I could get an experienced marketing manager in place, that alone would free up a lot of my time and generate much better sales and marketing collateral, of which we have almost none right now. That could deliver a triple whammy: free up my time, produce better sales and marketing collateral, and help generate new business.'

'Sounds like a no-brainer to me. What else jumps out at you?'

Howard was on a roll. He was immersed in his chart. 'The chart makes it clear just how much the business relies on Josh. He is the lynchpin in the back office. I'd like to pass all the financial management tasks over to him. He's an Excel guru, a mathematician; he loves the detail and probably has as much insight into the finances of the business as me.'

'Are there any other jobs, or even individual tasks, that aren't being done right now?' asked Joel.

'Well, honestly I don't know. For example, when I stepped back, I handed over all my sales tasks to Nigel. I assume he's been managing the renewals and building a pipeline of prospective business.'

'Why do you assume that?'

Howard was shocked by the question. 'Well, we are generating some revenue, after all!'

'But you're not *growing* your revenue. I'd suggest you make it a priority to check what's being done and by whom. You need to get to London – and soon. This is what it means to take ownership.'

Howard nodded and added 'book flights' to his growing list of To-Dos.

'When you come back from the UK, you'll have new insights

and we can begin the next step – which is to create clear job descriptions for each role.'

Howard looked at the whiteboard again and made a few more notes in his pad. He then looked up at Joel. 'So here's what I'm going to do,' he said. 'First I'll go to Hong Kong to inspire my shareholders to invest more funds and give us some breathing room. Then I'll go on to London to fire Nigel, followed by Israel to get Josh on board with the new structure and enrol him in taking over the financial management tasks. Then I'll come back to work on job descriptions.'

'Sounds like a plan,' said Joel.

Howard booked his flights, spent a few days of quality time with his family and then set off.

In Hong Kong, his co-directors and shareholders agreed to lend the business £50,000 based on the new business plan and Howard's willingness to spend the majority of his time in London.

His next task was to meet with Nigel. Presumably sensing what was coming, and even before Howard had ordered his double tall cappuccino in the Holborn Viaduct Starbucks, Nigel offered his resignation. Howard readily accepted it and then headed to Jerusalem for a meeting with Josh. Howard laid out how he intended to take back ownership and rebuild the business. He explained his intended reorganisation and relaunch – and Josh agreed to engage in the process.

Returning to London, Howard dived right back into work

with the London sales team, all of whom were surprisingly delighted and relieved to see Nigel gone and receive some clear and focused leadership. He began by inviting the staff, one by one, in private, to share their perspectives on how things had been and what they were feeling. It became instantly obvious that no one knew what they were supposed to be doing. There were no clear, assigned responsibilities. Howard had asked Nigel to make sure that all client accounts were assigned to specific salespeople. Nigel said he agreed, but had actually just ignored the direction. He had told the staff that everyone was responsible for every client and they should just follow his lead. As a result, everyone sat back and relied on Nigel who did nothing but shmooze with the same few clients. So there was no proactive sales activity. Unless a client called up with a problem or complained, they never heard from anyone at VinciWorks.

Howard immediately recognised the huge risk this represented. The company had no idea whether a client would cancel or renew until they paid, cancelled or complained about the renewal invoice. And there was virtually no upselling or cross-selling to existing clients. Nigel had been focused on the top eight or so large firms, but the other 140 were essentially ignored. Just as worrying was the fact that there was no prospecting for new business at all! New business only occurred if someone *happened* to call up.

Howard phoned Joel. 'It's a nightmare. It's actually worse than I thought. No one knows what they're supposed to be doing. There's no renewals process, no prospecting system, we're not talking to our clients. I now understand why the buyers reduced their offer. I wouldn't have bought the business either!'

'I'm not surprised,' said Joel. 'In many organisations that I see, there's little relationship between one's official title and the tasks they're supposed to perform. A "manager", for example, is often just someone with a little more experience and responsibility, but they're typically not actually managing others – that is to say, holding people accountable for results. So the fact that Nigel, as Managing Director, wasn't actually managing anyone is disappointing and upsetting, but not unusual.'

'What do I do?' asked Howard.

'The organisational chart was the first step. Now you need to create some clarity around the results you want each of your people to achieve in their jobs – starting with your sales team. And to do that, we'll need to create their job descriptions.'

SUMMARY

ORGANISATIONAL STRUCTURE

» To empower your people to deliver the results you desire, people need organisation – especially as your business grows.

» This is why you need a clear, structural picture of the key jobs that must take place in every area of your business, who's responsible for doing them and who reports to whom.

» Your organisational structure is best embodied in an organisational chart – a hierarchical grouping of linked boxes with job titles and names of relevant staff members in each box.

» An organisational chart enables you to objectively assess whether the right jobs are getting done, and whether the right people are doing them.

» It also helps you to see the various jobs that you're currently operating, empowering you to make deliberate, strategic decisions about which jobs you *want* to do and which you'd like to *delegate* to others.

» There are four key steps to creating an organisational chart:

(1) Define the *tasks* that must get done in each area of your business. (Hint: start by breaking down your business into its core task areas, and then list the tasks in each area):

- Guiding the business (i.e. entrepreneurial tasks);
- Managing the business (i.e. managerial tasks);
- Getting the business (i.e. sales and marketing tasks);
- Doing the business (i.e. production and delivery tasks); and
- Supporting the business (i.e. administration and finance tasks).

(2) Group those tasks into *jobs*. (Hint: If they relate to a similar skillset and they could all be done by one person, it's usually a single job.)

(3) Decide *who's* responsible for each job.

(4) Consider which jobs need to be *filled or changed* to help you realise your vision.

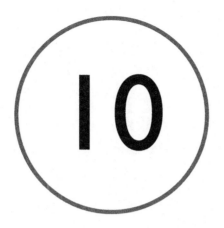

GETTING STRUCTURED

Howard and Joel organised an online meeting via Skype as Howard was still in London.

'Now that I've clarified my organisational structure, should we move on to the marketing strategy?' asked Howard.

'Absolutely, but not yet. We first need to create your job descriptions.'

'Doesn't my organisational chart do that?'

'Okay, let's back up a moment. Your organisational chart goes a long way towards fostering coordinated, organised action in pursuit of your vision. It identifies the various jobs that need to get done, and then assigns them to people, which helps to create role clarity and accountability. When people are clear on which job, or jobs, they're accountable for, they're more focused, less confused and more productive. Which ultimately means they achieve better results. So you're right. Your organisational chart helps a lot. But simply allocating a job to someone, and hoping for the best, isn't enough on its own. To achieve genuine role clarity and account-ability – and the focused action that goes with it – you need to define exactly what's expected in each job.'

'Experienced people should know what to do, shouldn't they?' said Howard.

'Yes and no. It's not uncommon for business owners to literally tear their hair out as they watch their staff fail to meet seemingly obvious expectations. If you're fulfilling an order, it's obvious that you should double-check the order documents to make sure they're accurate. That's just common sense, right?'

'Right,' said Howard.

'Well, I've got news for you: it might make sense *to you*, but that doesn't mean it's common practice for others. Humans make decisions, and then act, based on our expectations and assumptions of the world around us. If we assume we're expected to act in a certain way in a certain situation, we're likely to do so.'

'Yes, Aryeh taught me that already,' said Howard.

'So you'll know what the problem is then: our assumptions and expectations are based on many factors, including our past experience, our intuition, our personality characteristics and cues from our environment. And because each of us has a different background and personality, in the absence of clear cues from our environment, we often make different assumptions about what's expected. Even in relation to seemingly obvious tasks.'

'I hate to break it to you, Joel, but I can't exactly change people's past experience or personality.'

'No, but you *can* provide them with powerful environmental cues that will positively influence their daily decisions and actions. One cue for aligning your staff around a common understanding of what's expected is a clear job description for each role in your organisational structure.'

'I actually did create a job description of sorts for Josh when he took on the COO role. But we never did anything with it.'

'Do you have it handy? I'd like to see it.'

Howard searched for it on his laptop and shared his Skype screen with Joel. Joel studied the document for a little while. His face contorted slightly in the video window, as if he'd just sucked on a lemon.

'Is it that bad?' Howard asked.

Joel smiled, realising that his face had betrayed his thoughts. 'It's not *that* bad, but you have made a classic error. Perhaps the most critical aspect of an effective job description is that it must describe the *job*. It sounds absurd to even bother mentioning it, but your COO job description doesn't actually describe the job – at least not properly. It describes what Josh is *currently* doing, not what *needs* to be done to fulfil the requirements of the COO job.'

'Say that again ... I'm not sure I follow.'

'Most job descriptions are *people-focused*, not *job-focused*. And yours is no exception. It's tailored to the particular skills or interests of Josh, rather than what the job itself requires. You've effectively said: *I know I have this job here called chief operations officer, but Josh actually does so much more than that. I'll write a job description that describes everything he does or will do, including some finance tasks and customer service duties and whatever else I want him to do.* Can you see the problem here?'

Howard nodded, pretending that it was crystal clear but hoping that Joel would clarify it further.

'Put it this way: your organisational chart depicts the essential jobs or functions required to achieve your vision, but when you distort the descriptions of the jobs in that structure, you destroy the structural integrity and logical division of accountabilities you worked to create. That's a bad idea. It keeps you on the path of people-dependency. Accountabilities go with the job, not the person. Josh could well hold multiple jobs within the organisational structure, and that's fine. But be careful of randomly lumping everything into one job to fit Josh.'

'I guess that makes sense. Based on the organisational chart, Josh should really be holding a few different jobs – and each of those jobs needs a separate job description.'

'Exactly.'

'Is there anything else wrong with the document?' asked Howard, knowing full well that there would be.

'Yes, the second key problem is that it's not *results-focused*. It's simply a to-do list of the tasks for which Josh is responsible.'

'What's wrong with that?'

'A simple task list without describing the results that justify the tasks can have an unintended effect. It can build in restrictions and limitations. People can point to it as a reason *not* to do something. "That's not in my job description," they say.'

'I hear people saying that to me all the time, even without a job description!' said Howard.

'That's why I recommend starting each job description with an explicit statement of the results or outcomes that are expected. It removes limitations and opens up the role. It's not just a to-do list of tasks; it's an agreement to assume accountability for certain results. And that's a fundamentally different way of thinking. It means that simply doing what is asked isn't enough if you don't achieve the desired outcome.'

'I've never thought of it like that. As the owner, I'm always thinking about results – otherwise my family and I won't eat. But I guess my staff don't think of it in that way.'

'Right. And equally important is the fact that results statements let everyone know how the business benefits from the role. Staff can see how their position fits into the overall business vision. Each role, from the CEO to front-line staff, is linked by an integrated set of results that must be achieved for the business to achieve its goals. Seeing one's role in this broader context has a profound impact on motivation and commitment.'

'Can we develop an actual job description together, as a way of showing me how this works in practice?' asked Howard.

'Absolutely. You mentioned there was confusion among the sales team about their role. Why don't we start with the sales representative job?'

'Okay. And then maybe we can come back and re-do the COO job, too.'

'Fine by me. Now, building on what we've just discussed, an effective job description has three components: (1) A job objective; (2) Performance targets; and (3) Job tasks. Let's start by developing a clear and compelling job objective — that is, a statement about why the job exists; its underlying purpose. What do you think is the objective of a sales rep?'

'To make sales calls,' said Howard.

1 : A JOB OBJECTIVE

'See, that's where we differ. I'd say the objective *isn't* to make sales calls at all. That may be an important task, but it's not the reason for the job. The job's real objective is *to increase sales.* Or, put more comprehensively, to increase sales while growing profitable, long-term client relationships. Can you see the difference? One is about the tasks; the other is about outcomes and results. Someone can make calls all day, but if they're not increasing profitable sales and developing long-term customer relationships, they're not truly fulfilling the job.'

'Hang on. How does a sales rep influence profit?'

'If they have discretion around margin and are allowed to

offer discounts, that would influence profit. And if they're spending too much time on low-value customers, that would also influence profit.'

'Okay, that makes sense. I like the idea of focusing staff on results. Keep going ...'

2: PERFORMANCE TARGETS

'The next component is performance targets. Just as the overall business needs defined performance targets to help track progress towards the big-picture vision, so too does each job require ways of measuring whether its objectives are being achieved. The most effective job descriptions clearly articulate what successful performance looks like. For example, if the objective of a sales rep is to "grow profitable, long-term client relationships", what performance targets might you set?'

'Umm ... how about percentage of annual renewals on individual accounts?' said Howard. 'Or value of up-sales? Or maybe number and value of new clients?'

'They're all good examples. Write them down. Of course, targets don't just relate to tangible, easy-to-quantify amounts expressed in pounds or dollars and percentages. They could relate to whether performance meets certain quality standards, timely completion of tasks or even whether behaviour is consistent with your company values. Can you think of any non-monetary standards?'

'The quality of their relationship with their key accounts is critical. You could measure that by how often they "touch" the client by phone, email or in person. We need to build relationships with our customers because this leads to new business, particularly when that person leaves and joins a new company. If the relationship is good, they almost always call us and ask us to pitch.'

'Great work. Any other targets?'

'I'd really like to put a timeframe on the sales targets,' said Howard. 'They could be quarterly targets for example, and I could give them a quarterly bonus if they hit it, which would create an additional incentive. Also, I've always felt that clients should never wait more than 24 hours for a reply, even if it's just an acknowledgement that we'll get back to them with a full response. It amazes me that some of our salespeople just don't get it.'

'It's like we said before: people have different assumptions around what's acceptable. That's why you need to clarify it for them. Sorry to harp on this point, but this is what it means to take *ownership*.'

'This all sounds great in theory. I'm just not sure that implementing it will be so simple …'

3: JOB TASKS

'Just a second. There's one last component: the job tasks. The good news is that you've already defined them in your organisational structure. They're the specific tasks or activities that each jobholder will handle day-to-day. Once you've clarified that, your job description is complete. Now your task is to go through this process for each job in your structure. But I'd suggest you start with the sales team, and ask Josh to do the same for the operational side of the business. You'll just need to fix Josh's job description first.'

'So who'll do my job description then?' asked Howard.

'That's part of my job. I'll help you work on the CEO job description, and you can then present it to your board for approval.'

'Okay, that sounds good. But I have to say that all of this opens up a whole can of worms around implementation. For example, it means I need to have a way to work out if people are actually hitting their targets. Like my sales team. How will I know if they're meeting clients, closing business, and that the business they are closing is profitable? This is really embarrassing to say, but I cannot honestly tell you whether the business is profitable, let alone at an individual product or contract level.

'Since I started, I've been running the company bank account as my personal piggy bank and I don't differentiate between legitimate company expenses and my personal expenses. So how can I determine profit? I don't even take a formal salary. I just take whatever I need to pay my bills. I really have no idea what our current cash flow situation is on a month-to-month or week-to-week basis. Which means I actually have no idea if we're making or losing money. All I know is how much is in the bank account.'

'Howard, that's not unusual,' said Joel. 'It's rare to come across a small business that manages its finances effectively. You weren't trained in accountancy, you don't employ a proper accountant, so

I'm not surprised by the lack of accountability. Either way, this is clearly a key area for us to focus on. I typically recommend working on the most critical and urgent systems first – the ones that are most likely to affect your immediate results. We started with your collections system, which helped your cash flow, but clearly the next system to work on is your financial reporting. Every business needs real-time, accurate insight into their financial position. We can also set up a budgeting system to help you plan your cash flow, measure and report on your actual results, and compare those against your forecast.'

'That would be incredible.'

'But let's not get ahead of ourselves,' said Joel. 'First, create the job descriptions.'

SUMMARY

JOB DESCRIPTIONS

» To achieve genuine role clarity and accountability – and the focused action that goes with it – you'll need to define exactly what's expected in each job in your organisational structure.

» An effective *job description* has three key components:

(1) A **job objective** – a statement about why the job exists; its underlying purpose.

(2) **Performance targets** – ways of measuring whether the objective is being achieved (including tangible, quantity targets like amount of widgets produced or revenue generated, and/or quality targets like timely completion of tasks or adherence to company values).

(3) **Job tasks** – the specific tasks or activities that the job-holder will handle day-to-day to achieve their targets and the job objectives.

FREE RESOURCES: To download concise summaries, templates and resources to help you apply the principles in this chapter, go to www.mindfulentrepreneur.co/resources

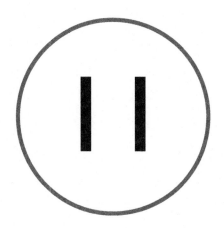

BUILDING
ACCOUNTABILITY

Over the next couple of months, Howard worked hard to complete all the job descriptions. With Joel's help, he also empowered Josh to delve deeply into VinciWorks' finances, creating an impressive Excel-based financial reporting system that provided real-time insight and accountability. Howard could now forecast his profit and cash flow, and see how he was tracking against his forecast.

'All the financial reports are updated in real-time and saved in Dropbox, so I can check our position wherever and whenever I want,' Howard told Joel when they next met. 'It's a great feeling but it's also a bit scary.'

'I'm glad it's up and running, but why is it scary?' asked Joel.

'Now that I actually know what's going on, there really are NO EXCUSES!' They both laughed at the irony. 'But seriously, although the numbers are now available, sometimes I don't want to look at them. Take a look. You can see that cash is still really tight. In fact, I've actually imposed a reduced and fixed monthly limit on my own drawings. I know it's necessary, but it hurts.'

'Don't worry, we'll work on marketing strategies to boost revenue and cash flow soon; we've just got a little more to do on getting things organised and systematised first.'

'I actually have a question for you about systems. In general, they're having a positive effect, but I've been facing some resistance from some of my staff when it comes to implementing the systems.'

'Go on,' said Joel, 'what's the specific issue?'

'Josh has been amazing with the tracking and reporting on all sorts of numbers. Not only do I know how much we're spending each month and on what items, but I can also see how much revenue is being generated by each sales rep, from which products and from which clients.'

'Fantastic. That's exactly the kind of insight and accountability you need to drive performance. But I still don't understand …'

'Hard data like sales numbers are easy to track. But tracking less quantifiable information is another story. For example, I'm struggling to track and create accountability around whether our sales reps are maintaining the right kind of relationship with their customers. We have a cloud-based database for entering and managing all customer information. It was relatively inexpensive, and it should be able to give us a detailed picture of how often the salespeople are "touching" their clients. That was one of the key performance targets in the sales rep job description. But the problem is, the sales reps are not entering the data into the database – at least not consistently or in a timely manner. So it's "rubbish in, rubbish out", as they say.'

'This is a crucial point,' said Joel. 'You can build all the systems in the world, but if your staff don't apply them, you'll never achieve the results. Inputting data into the database is just another system and systems *implementation* is critical to success.'

'Yes, I can see that already. I just didn't view "customer data input" as another system.'

'It is. Every recurring task in your business is a system – and you can either define them and hold people accountable, or let them go and leave it to chance.'

'How do I deal with the accountability component? I can add inputting data into the database as a mandatory requirement in each sales job description, but is that enough?'

'I'd recommend going even further. Step one is to define and document the system clearly, like we did for your collections system. But you also need to create a *culture* in which everyone knows that applying the designated systems is mandatory. You've expended a lot of time and energy in creating these systems. If you don't enforce them, it'll be a wasted effort.'

'I don't want to come across as heavy-handed,' said Howard,

'like I'm walking around with a stick ready to punish people who aren't following the systems. That's not the kind of culture I want.'

'You know, it's interesting. I find that where there are clearly understood and well-enforced rules of engagement, you don't have to discipline people nearly as often. But where the rules are merely seen as recommendations that aren't enforced by management, people are *less* likely to follow them. Which means you end up having to act as the policeman *more* often.'

'Are you saying that I need to make consistent failure to follow systems a dismissible offence?' asked Howard. 'Follow the process or follow the exit sign?'

'In short, yes. But that's a little simplistic. Dismissal should be a last resort – and one that forms part of a broader performance management and accountability strategy. For example, you should be setting up two kinds of regular meetings with your staff to review their performance and give them constructive feedback on issues that arise – like not following systems, for example. That process must be in place and operating effectively well before you consider dismissal.'

'What kinds of meetings do you suggest?'

'First of all, regular team meetings. Take your sales team, for example. You should be meeting them every week to review their progress against targets, plan the week or two ahead and make sure they're following the systems, such as using the database. But you shouldn't stop there. It's also critical to set up regular weekly or fortnightly meetings with *each* member of staff who reports to you.'

'Really? With every direct report?'

'Yes, and each of your direct reports should do the same with their direct reports – if they have any, that is – throughout the entire organisation. Accountability is driven by two factors: having the right data to measure performance, and having regular meetings with people to encourage and coach around that performance. You don't have to operate all the systems yourself, but taking ownership requires you to care enough to ensure they're being implemented.'

'We've actually been talking about scheduling regular sales meetings for a while. I can certainly make that happen; I think the team will appreciate it. I just need to make sure that the meetings are productive rather than just an enjoyable talk-fest.'

'I can teach you how to run effective meetings. It won't surprise you to know that there's a system for that, too. But let's discuss it in our next meeting; it'll take us some time.'

'Sure. Can I raise another issue that's been bothering me, though?'

'Of course,' said Joel.

'Creating the job descriptions and then documenting and implementing systems is tedious work. The more I do, the more I learn; and the more I learn, the more I realise there is to do. You need to create a method or a tool to help speed up the process for people like me. I'd buy it!'

Joel smiled knowingly. 'Actually, that's part of what I'm planning to create as I scale my own business. I want to reach more people *and* I want to offer a solution that makes it easier to write job descriptions, design systems and generally achieve results faster. That said, I'm afraid there's no silver bullet. It will always take *some* work on the part of the owner. It's that *ownership* concept again.'

'Talking about ownership, when you initially came to my office, you were looking for advice on scaling your own coaching practice through online technology. Is that still on the cards? Is that how you want to deliver this new, easier, faster process?'

'In short, yes. And I'd love your feedback when you have time. I haven't wanted to bother you with it over the last few months. I've been focused on making *your* business a success story before turning to mine.'

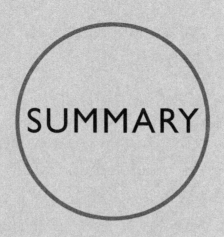

SUMMARY

BUILDING ACCOUNTABILITY

» Every recurring task in your business is a system – and you can either define those systems and hold people accountable for them, or let them go and leave it to chance.

» Effective systems implementation requires you to create a culture of accountability in which everyone knows that following the systems is mandatory.

» To create that culture, you need a two-part accountability strategy: (1) ensuring access to the right data to measure performance (e.g. via a client relationship management database, financial reports, etc.); and (2) regular meetings to encourage and coach around that performance.

» Business owners should implement two key kinds of meetings:

1. Regular weekly or fortnightly team meetings to review the team's progress against targets, plan the week ahead and make sure they're following systems; and
2. Regular weekly or fortnightly meetings with each direct report (with each direct report doing the same for their own direct reports).

» Real *ownership* means caring enough to follow up on your systems and the results they produce.

FREE RESOURCES: To download concise summaries, templates and resources to help you apply the principles in this chapter, go to www.mindfulentrepreneur.co/resources

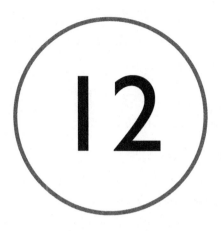

FINDING BALANCE

Howard and Aryeh began to meet on a more regular basis. Howard found it quite therapeutic and Aryeh was more than happy to share his wisdom.

'I'm enjoying work at the moment,' said Howard one day. 'I'm engaged and excited by the progress we're making. I'm finally leading the business, I'm moving towards my purpose and I'm starting to see results.'

'That's wonderful, Howard, I'm really happy for you.'

'It's not *all* good, though.'

'What do you mean?'

'I'm focusing on work almost to the exclusion of everything else. Andrea wants more of my time and, although the kids don't say it to me, I know I'm not there for them enough. My family is so important to me and I'm wondering if improving the business is becoming a bit of a drug.'

'The fact that you're aware of this issue is fantastic,' said Aryeh.

Howard was surprised. 'What's fantastic about that?'

'It shows that you've become more mindful. You're aware of the problem. And once you're aware of a problem, you can do something to fix it.'

'I'm not sure what to do, though. If I take my foot off the pedal and stop driving the business, it may lose the momentum we've built. It's not yet ready to run without me.'

'I understand that,' said Aryeh. 'Let me make some general points and then we can try to apply it to your situation.

'First of all, your business isn't a separate part of your life; it's part of an integrated whole. And if you're out of alignment in one area, you won't experience the holistic meaning and fulfilment you desire. In practical terms, this means you need to give expression to your purpose in a balanced way, in each area of your life. This encompasses your relationship with yourself, including your physical, emotional and spiritual health and wellbeing; your relationship with others, including family and friends; and your relationship with the world, including your business and any communal or non-paid work. You've started with your business, which is all about your impact on the world. Now you need to look at the other two areas.'

'Yes, I feel that. I'm just not sure how to make it all work.'

'I find it helpful to take three simple steps: (1) Define your values; (2) Set goals; and (3) Create action plans. The good news is that you've already completed the first step. Remember that exercise when you wrote your funeral speech?'

1: DEFINE YOUR VALUES

Howard thought back to the first time he had spoken with Aryeh. It seemed like a lifetime ago. Aryeh had helped him to articulate his values and capture them in a core purpose statement.

'Yes, I remember. You took me from my own funeral to "creating the greatest sustainable value – no excuses!". I have truly been trying to live that core purpose.'

'Right,' said Aryeh. 'But you've been focusing exclusively on one area of your life: your work. Now you need to apply that same energy to fulfilling your core purpose in the other areas, too. As I said, it's about taking a holistic, balanced approach.'

'I know we're supposed to live a balanced life but what does that mean practically?'

'It means setting goals for *each* area and devising an action plan to achieve those goals.'

2: SET GOALS

'So you essentially want me to write a business plan, but for my whole life?' Howard asked. 'Perhaps I should have done that first before committing to focus on saving and building my business?'

'Ideally, yes. But in your case, given the urgency of your work situation and its impact on you and others, it was important to stabilise that area before you turned to other aspects of your life. You were in a pretty dark place when we first met.'

Howard recalled the 3 a.m. nightmares, the thoughts of life insurance, and the sense of helplessness.

'The business is still fragile. The risks are still there, failure is still a possibility and there's still so much work to do. But things have definitely improved and I'm in a much better place than I was when we first met.'

'Good, so let's begin. We'll start with setting goals for your relationships with *yourself*.'

'Do you mean my health?'

'Broadly speaking, yes. On the physical side, it might include goals like implementing an eating regime that will help you lose a few kilograms or committing to go to the gym once or twice a week. For some people, it might even include a goal like running a marathon. It's up to you.'

'For a long time I've wanted to get back to my fighting weight of 75 kilograms.'

'You were a fighter?' asked Aryeh.

'Yes, I was a black belt in karate. And now that you mention it, a second goal would be to get back into the dojo and be fit enough to teach again.'

'Great goals. Your physical wellbeing is important, but it's also worth considering your emotional and spiritual health. Nourishing our emotional and spiritual side helps us cope with challenges and live with more fulfilment. Remember, this is a holistic approach. What goals would you like to set on that front?'

'What do you mean? I'm feeling pretty good right now.'

'That's great to hear, but do you remember that morning in your accountant's office?'

'The day of the ambush?' asked Howard, the colour draining from his cheeks.

'Yes, that day. You have to expect that life will continue to provide opportunities to learn and to grow. It'll continue to throw challenges your way. You need to be able to deal with situations like that and, as far as possible, remain emotionally centred.'

'So what do you suggest?'

'There are many ways to maintain your emotional equilibrium and contribute to your sense of fulfilment. For example, I find meditating to be essential for my wellbeing. For other people, taking a yoga class may be helpful. Others like to read a novel or a personal-growth book every other month. Even just taking a walk each morning to clear your mind can be helpful. There are a lot of options open to you.'

'Someone mentioned a meditation app the other day. How about I start by downloading that?'

'That'd be good,' said Aryeh. 'At some stage, let's talk about meditation in more detail, because it's a powerful approach. But for now, just start by using the app for five to ten minutes a day.'

'Yeah, I could do that.'

'As you begin to manage your relationship with yourself, you'll also find it easier to manage your relationships with others.'

'Who do you mean by *others*?' asked Howard.

'Your family and friends. When you articulated your values in your funeral speech, for example, you mentioned having amazing kids whom you love and who love you.'

'Yeah, I also said I'd be the coolest of all dads, and build and maintain a great marriage.'

'I'm glad you remember,' said Aryeh. 'So what goals would you like to set to express those values?'

Howard sat back, pondered and then began. 'A good starting point would be to spend more time in the same country as the rest of my family. And if that's not possible right now, at the very least to communicate with each of them more regularly. I hate to admit this, but on some trips I get so absorbed in the business that I forget about the family. I don't want that. I want to remain conscious of them, of what's happening in their lives, and to always remember how important they are to me.'

'That's nice and it's a good start,' said Aryeh. 'But I think you need to set goals that are more practical and specific. When you set goals in your business plan, I'm guessing you included specific numbers and timelines, right?'

'Yes, of course,' said Howard.

'Well, why treat your family differently?'

Howard was silent for a minute while he tried to think of measurable personal goals. 'As you know, I'm currently spending more time overseas than I spend at home. But Andrea and the kids agree that right now I have to do this to rebuild the business. We discussed this and we all agreed that it was necessary.'

'Yes, but there's still a cost to the relationships, whether they agree or not. How about setting a maximum number of days or weeks that you'll be away and a minimum amount of time to be at home?'

'You mean like committing to live in same country as my family no less than 75 per cent of the time?'

'Yes, exactly – if that's practical. Or you could aim not to be away from the family for more than four weeks at a time.'

'Flying time and changing time zones means that I lose three days each trip. Can we negotiate? How about I target not being away for more than six weeks at a time?'

'Well, if we're negotiating, how about also committing to stay home for at least two weeks each time you do come back?'

'Yes, I guess I could do that, too,' said Howard. While he knew these goals represented relatively minor adjustments to his schedule, he felt somehow soothed by the idea of making concrete, measurable commitments to his own needs and to those of his family. He was excited to share them with Andrea and the kids, knowing they would recognise his decisions as a shift that honoured them and the family as a whole.

'The last area is your relationship with the world – beyond yourself and beyond your family. For many people, this is primarily about their work – their income-generating business or job. And you've already set goals for this in your business plan. But many people extend this area even further, to activities like non-paid work and volunteering.'

'I used to be involved in supporting and even leading a small charity. I loved it. There was something really satisfying about helping a community in that way. But I chose to let it go once I knew I'd have to focus so much of my time on the business.'

'As long as you're making the decision intentionally, mindfully, that's okay,' said Aryeh. 'Once the business settles down, you can always revisit this area.' He paused before continuing. 'We've covered a lot of ground today. Can I set you some homework? Otherwise it's all theory.'

'Sure. What do you want me to do?'

3: CREATE ACTION PLANS

'Create some action plans. For each goal you set in each area of your life, write down exactly what steps you'll take over the next 90 days to make those goals a reality. Then set dates by when you'll complete each step. The idea is that every 90 days, you'll review your progress and set new goals for the next period.'

'Wow, you sound more and more like Joel: "Design a system and write it down, including measurable targets such as dates or amounts!" I'll give it a try and let you know how I go.'

SUMMARY

FINDING BALANCE

» Your business isn't a separate part of your life; it's part of an integrated whole.

» If you're out of alignment in one area, you may not experience the holistic meaning and fulfilment you desire.

» Instead, give expression to your core purpose in *each* area of your life, in a balanced way.

» You have three broad areas: your relationship with **yourself** (including your physical, emotional and spiritual health and wellbeing), with **others** (including family and friends) and with **the world** (which includes your business and any communal or non-paid work).

» To create balance, follow these three critical steps:

1. Define your **values** (Hint: you already defined them as you uncovered your core purpose);
2. Set measurable **goals** for *each* area of your life (e.g. lose 5 kilograms, go to the gym once or twice a week, read a novel or a personal-growth book every other month, etc.).
3. Create **action plans** to achieve those goals (outline what steps you'll take over the next 90 days to make the goals a reality and then set dates by when you'll complete each step).

FREE RESOURCES: To download concise summaries, templates and resources to help you apply the principles in this chapter, go to www.mindfulentrepreneur.co/resources

MARKETING
FOR GROWTH

It took several months, but Howard's decision to lose weight and regain his fitness had started to bear fruit. He was running at least three mornings a week, and he'd even found the courage to walk back into a Karate dojo and reconnect with the martial art he'd all but mastered while living in Hong Kong. The first few weeks were painful. He rediscovered muscles he forgot he had. But he was surprised at how quickly he began to feel fitter, stronger and healthier. He even felt more mentally alert and focused, and he was sleeping better, too.

With Andrea's support, he'd also cut down the carbohydrates in his diet, and was already 4 kilograms closer to his 75 kilogram target weight. And while he hadn't yet achieved his goal of being in the same country as his family at least 75 per cent of the time, he had made a concerted effort to not be away from home for more than six weeks at a time and to stay at home for at least two weeks each occasion he came back. Rather than diminishing his efforts to rebuild his business, the extra time at home actually helped him forge new opportunities in Australia. Overall, he noticed a deepening sense of wellbeing; it was a feeling that he hadn't experienced in a long time.

There was no doubt in Howard's mind that his ability to make these changes in his personal life was directly linked to the increased stability in and sense of control he had over his business. The money was being proactively managed and tracked against a budget, there were structures and systems in place around the sales force, and he had real-time visibility into their sales activities and engagement with clients. Consequently, he was feeling as optimistic about the future as he'd felt when he launched VinciWorks. In fact, he was quietly confident that if the team continued to do what they had agreed to do, they would show a modest profit for the year.

That's not to say it was always easy. But there was a palpably different atmosphere and mood across the business. It felt as though the culture had changed. The implementation of structure, job descriptions with clear targets, systems, accurate progress reports and regular meetings with open communication had given the team direction and clarity. Everyone knew what was expected of them, and how they were contributing to the success of the business as a whole.

Although initially sceptical, staff were gradually taking ownership of the business' purpose, too. Howard felt proud when he first heard one of the sales reps explaining to a client that 'VinciWorks' purpose is to create a safer, fairer and more honest world', and that 'we do it in a humble but important way by creating great compliance and risk-management tools'. At that moment, Howard experienced a direct connection between his personal core purpose and the purpose he had set for the business. It was satisfying and fulfilling in a way he hadn't previously experienced.

'I'm impressed,' said Joel, admiring the financial report on Howard's shared Skype screen during their fortnightly coaching session. 'Considering where you were not so long ago, this is a great result.'

'I agree, but my purpose is to create the *greatest* sustainable value, remember? The results are good, we've achieved a level of stability, but now it's time to really grow. I want to work on our marketing strategy.'

'Okay, let's flesh out the marketing strategy we outlined in your business plan. In essence, it's about giving effect to your vision. Do you remember how you described your five-year vision?'

'I have it written down here,' said Howard, pulling from his bag a sheet of A4 paper with his core purpose statement and his five-year vision printed in large bold type. He read aloud: 'VinciWorks will provide innovative online compliance training, risk-management software and consulting to at least 60 per cent of the top 1000 UK law firms and 500 of the UK's third- and fourth-tier accounting and banking businesses.'

'Good. So is that still the vision?'

'Yes, although I also see opportunities opening up in Australia and China in the risk software and consulting space.'

'Even if we stick with the original vision, it's still a big vision. It means you'll need to think very strategically about how to attract those customers, as well as how to satisfy them and entice them to come back. That's really what a marketing strategy is all about.'

'Go on,' said Howard.

'To build your customer base, you need to understand the process – the journey – your customers undertake when making their purchase decisions. While each customer is unique, in general, they all move through a six-step (partly unconscious) mental process. This holds true whether you're targeting large or small law firms, or expanding into the banking and accounting sectors. In all markets, the speed of your growth will depend on your ability to move prospects efficiently and effectively through this decision-making process.'

Joel showed Howard a simple diagram on his screen.

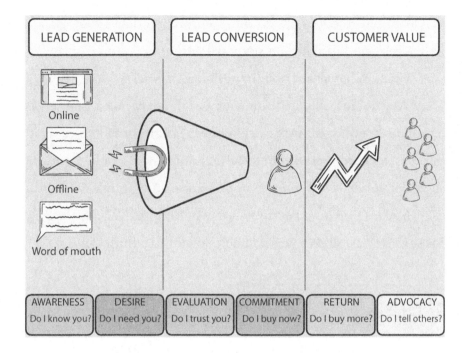

I : AWARENESS

'Let's explore each of these steps. First up is awareness. Nothing happens until someone becomes aware of you and your product or service. You might have the most impressive offering the world has ever seen, but if they don't know about you, you won't grow very fast. So the key is to select the marketing channels that most effectively reach *your* target market. If you're targeting third- and fourth-tier accounting firms and banks, for example, which channels do you think would reach them most effectively?'

'I'd love to put on compliance training events for law firms and a risk-management event for foreign banks in the UK. And we could use channels like the Law Society and ICAEW Association of Chartered Accountants to promote our products; they already have a relationship with our potential customers.'

'Great. What about online or digital channels?'

'We should really be more savvy in this area given that we *are* an online training business. I suppose LinkedIn could work as it's business-focused. People might also search for us online and we should invest in search engine optimisation and Google AdWords.'

'Make sure you write this all down,' said Joel. 'These are good ideas; there's no reason you couldn't do all these things in time.'

2: DESIRE

'Let's assume you're able to build awareness,' said Joel. 'The next step is creating desire. People only make buying decisions when they desire something enough. And people only desire something when it fulfils a real need or solves a real problem in their lives.'

'How do we get our customers to want or need what we're offering?' asked Howard.

'The reality is that we can't actually *create* the need for customers: they either have a need or they don't. But we *can* trigger a sense of desire by stimulating conscious needs or by helping customers become aware of latent, subconscious needs. And we do that through deliberately crafting the marketing messages we put into each channel. If they're expressed effectively in a way that speaks to customers' needs, it will cultivate a desire to take action.

'We don't have enough time right now to go into detail

around how to craft compelling marketing communications, so let's just identify the *types* of marketing communications you'll use to deliver those key messages – such as print ads, videos, website landing pages, email offers, flyers, and so on. Look at each of the channels you wrote down and ask: what resources do you need to get your message across in each channel?'

'If we're going to invest in SEO and run AdWords campaigns, we need to ensure our website looks good and contains all the information a prospect will need,' Howard said. 'And if we're running events and networking, we'll need some professional marketing materials like a decent brochure and a PowerPoint presentation.'

'You'll also need a company LinkedIn page and text for paid LinkedIn ads,' added Joel.

'We do have a LinkedIn page, but I should probably review what it says,' said Howard as he continued to note down the ideas.

3: EVALUATION

'The next step is building trust,' said Joel. 'In some cases, the movement from awareness to desire and commitment is almost instantaneous. Like buying gum at the checkout counter. But for purchases that are more expensive, risky or complicated – like your risk-management system, for example – most people need to engage in an evaluation process of some kind before they commit. They'll want to consider your solution carefully, and potentially weigh it against other solutions, to assess its relative value and determine whether they can trust your marketing claims.

'Take buying a car. Most would-be car buyers engage in extensive research online – with friends, mechanics, via magazine reviews and through test drives – before they make their decision. Why do you think that is?'

'I suppose it's just human nature that we don't commit to something unless we have some evidence that the benefits of taking action outweigh the risks,' said Howard.

'Right. And even where potential customers desire *a* solution to their problem, it doesn't necessarily mean they'll choose *your* solution. The reality is that people need to know if they can trust you and your solution first before they take action.'

'So how do you create trust, then? My sense is that people are less trusting of advertising campaigns than ever before.'

'That's exactly the point,' said Joel. 'Most customers have a somewhat cynical approach. They've been burned believing self-serving claims in brochures, flyers and TV ads. As a result, there's a paradigm shift going on in marketing today. It's called "content marketing".'

'I've heard of it, but I'm not exactly sure what it is or what it involves.'

'The central idea behind content marketing is simple but powerful: you create and distribute relevant, useful and engaging content to your target market for free ... *before you ask them to buy.* For example, informative blog articles on your site or others' sites, white papers, publications, videos, ebooks, free demonstrations, free consultations, webinars, group presentations and try-before-you-buy offers. That way, you give customers an opportunity to genuinely assess your credibility. And if your content is high quality, you'll build credibility and trust – and significantly increase the chances of winning them over as new customers.'

'We actually have a very extensive product brochure; we could dress that up a bit,' said Howard.

'There's nothing wrong with a product brochure. It can be very helpful. But a brochure is about selling your product. I'm not talking about sales. I'm talking about distributing *genuinely valuable* content. This is not some marketing trick – self-serving promotion dressed up as valuable content won't work. To build real credibility and trust, you'll need to earn it. Think of it this way: traditional advertising is *telling* the world you're a rock star; content marketing is *showing* the world that you are one. Which do you think is more persuasive?'

'Okay, I get it. But we may have an even more fundamental trust issue to overcome. After Nigel resigned, it seems he went to many of our key clients and spread a rumour that we were in financial trouble and probably wouldn't be around for much longer.'

'How might you rebuild trust then via content marketing?' asked Joel.

'We need to re-establish in the minds of our clients that we're stable and that we'll be around for a lot longer. It's incredible but next year will be ten years since I brought together the 14 large law firms and we launched the Online Compliance Consortium. So maybe we could publish a tenth anniversary, high-quality, glossy report with insights about the last ten years of compliance and how we see the future panning out. That could help reinforce our stability and position us as leaders in the industry. We could even get leading journalists, risk partners and heads of compliance from the top firms to contribute opinion pieces.'

'Great idea, provided it's truly informative rather than a sales pitch. Send it to everyone. And it could be downloaded from your website, in your email signatures, given away at your events. Also, since your clients live in the world of email, you could create a monthly compliance update that includes regulatory updates, blog articles on topical compliance issues, relevant case studies, and so on.'

'I'd love to do that,' said Howard. 'I've even thought about producing posters that reinforce the content from each of our compliance training courses. Clients could stick them up in the staff kitchen, around the water coolers and other gathering places to reinforce awareness of compliance. And we now have a marketing manager who could implement these ideas. This is really exciting. It feels like we're a real company.'

'You're on a roll, Howard. It's incredible how creative you can be when your mind is free to think about your business more strategically – when you can work *on* your business and not just *in* it. Keep going, though. Anything else?'

'If we really want to give away real value, we could repurpose some of the videos we create as introductory videos to the courses and put them up on YouTube. We could then send links to clients and prospects. Once prospects see the quality of our products, they are almost always satisfied that we can meet their needs.'

'In other words you create trust,' said Joel.

'Yes, I guess so. I just hadn't thought of it that way. Giving prospects access to some of the actual content would be a bit like offering them a test drive.'

4: COMMITMENT

Looking back at the long list of content marketing strategies, Joel said, 'I think we've enough trust-building ideas for now. Let's talk about gaining commitment. This is where the rubber meets the road. Creating awareness and building desire are all about generating leads and bringing prospects into your sphere of influence. Sharing valuable knowledge and providing opportunities to evaluate your offerings is about building trust. Inspiring commitment is about "lead conversion" or "sales". Put simply, it's about converting interested prospects into paying customers.'

'Now you're talking. I've been waiting for this part of the puzzle. I always say to my staff that it's not closed till it's closed. Bringing prospects to the water is one thing, but getting them to drink is another. This is what it's all about.'

'Sorry, Howard, but I only partly agree. It's true that the commitment stage is where the sale is made. But the real work is in the preceding stages. If you've done a good job of creating awareness, building desire and fostering trust, you'll inspire a commitment to buy.'

'So do I simply twiddle my thumbs and wait for commitment to happen?'

'You're a tough audience, Howard,' said Joel. 'Of course, you'll still need to invite commitment proactively and, where necessary, deal with any customer concerns that arise as they're evaluating your offerings.'

'How do I do that?'

'There's no limit to the ways in which you can inspire commitment. You can create urgency by making limited-time offers or lower the risk by offering a money-back guarantee. You could also continue to build trust by making entry-level, low-cost offers before you ask for a larger commitment, or use the principle of scarcity if there's limited supply of your offering. Like those prompts on hotel and airline booking sites that say "only ten seats left". I don't know if they're true, but they certainly work. Can you think of other ways in which you might use some of these strategies?'

'We don't do any of those things right now; I don't like trying to scare or threaten customers,' Howard said. 'I sometimes make them aware of upcoming price rises to motivate them, but not in any systematic way.'

'Hang on. It's not about scaring people into buying. It's about lowering the risk for people to make a decision. Free trials and lower-cost, entry-level offers, for instance, allow customers to experience the product before upgrading to the full solution.'

Howard considered the idea for a while before responding. 'We've got a basic version of our Learning Management System (LMS) that we give away for free because the clients need it to manage the online courses we sell to them. Although the basic LMS is free, the goal is to upsell clients to the more feature-rich versions. This works well. But I've never thought about this in relation to our Risk Management System. We only have a full-feature, Rolls Royce version. Perhaps there's a market for a basic, entry-level version for firms that aren't sophisticated enough or don't have enough budget for the full system?'

'That's exactly what I'm talking about. It's much easier to have them initially commit to a smaller investment and then later upgrade when they truly understand and have experienced the value.'

'I need to think about this. It makes sense, but it's going to take time and money to dummy down the full system.'

'Don't expect to be able to implement all these ideas at once. We'll add it to the list and come back to it when we decide what to implement now and what to leave until later.'

'That's a relief. What's the next step?'

5: RETURN

'The next step is return. Driving customers to your business is one thing; keeping them and growing your relationship with them is another. And since it's five to ten times cheaper to keep a customer than to acquire a new one, you'll need to get this right. Software as a Service (SaaS) businesses like VinciWorks are often valued based on the lifetime value of a client. That's their total spend over the number of years they stay with you, so this is particularly important to you.'

'I learned this lesson during the Global Financial Crisis,' said Howard. 'In October 2008, Lehman Brothers went bust, sending a massive shockwave around the world. The legal sector had been riding the boom for years, bought new buildings, expanded their operations and borrowed lots of money to do so. When the crash came, they were exposed and almost every law firm stopped spending money.

'Prior to October 2008, we had been closing three or four new firms a month. But almost overnight, it stopped. All pending deals froze and it became obvious that for the time being we couldn't expect to sign any new business. It was really frightening how overnight VinciWorks went from solid growth to the verge of collapse. Our only hope was to ensure that our current clients renewed. We could potentially survive on renewal income, but if that started to decline, the business was dead.'

'What did you do?' asked Joel.

'I moved us out of our London office, we shed staff and just hunkered down to see what would happen. Over the next three months, renewals remained constant.'

'Sounds like a tough time. Did you do anything specific to maintain renewal rates?'

'A lot. We reprioritised and made our existing customer

relationships our single most important focus. Nigel spent all day every day visiting existing clients and ensuring they were happy with our service. We also began to invest in improving the product and responding to product enhancement requests more quickly. We invested in rebuilding our Learning Management System from scratch and upgraded all our clients to the new system at no additional charge. This reinforced our value to our clients.'

'I'm impressed. That's exactly what I'm talking about. What about your contracts? Did you discount for extended renewal terms?'

'Yes, we did do that and it worked. We offered a 15 per cent discount if a customer signed and paid for three years in advance. But because we didn't have the systems and controls in place, and didn't manage our cash flow, by the beginning of the third year, we'd already spent the revenue relating to that year. I actually think that was the beginning of the cash-flow problems that you helped us resolve.'

'I think it's worth revisiting the three-year contract offer now that you have better systems in place.'

'No, I don't think so. Our own quality standard demands that we deliver a product that clients want to renew every year.'

'That's a powerful message. A hybrid option might be to sign three-year deals but have clients pay at the start of each year.'

'Yes, with an option to cancel,' said Howard.

'What else can you do to convey the value you're providing? You said you've focused on improving the product but are you telling customers what you've done for them?'

'We could easily send out product updates. We already have the data written up as part of our product development system.'

Joel recorded the idea, and continued to fire questions at Howard. 'I understand that you have a high renewal rate, but do you do anything to identify high-risk clients? Clients who may be at risk of leaving?'

'What do you mean?' asked Howard.

'Well, how would you know if a client is at risk of not renewing?'

'I suppose if they're not using the products, they're not getting value from them, which means they may be at risk. But I don't really track that in any way.'

'Could you?' asked Joel.

'It's just pulling data that's already in our system. It's not hard to do. And come to think of it, it's a good idea. We can definitely implement that one quickly and easily.'

'Excellent. And that data will help you not only save high-risk accounts but also grow your existing accounts.'

'How?'

'What are you currently doing to grow your revenues via upselling or cross-selling other products or services?' asked Joel.

'We invest most of our time in renewals and haven't focused much on upselling or cross-selling. When we do, it's usually just reacting to a client request rather than doing anything proactive.'

'If you regularly reviewed your client usage data to identify the products you could upsell or cross-sell to them, I'd be surprised if it didn't become a huge opportunity for new revenue.'

'I could get Josh to put in place a monthly reporting system to review both high-risk accounts and high-usage accounts who might be ready for other products.'

'Great idea, Howard. Soon you'll be teaching me!'

6: ADVOCACY

'Okay, just one more step and then we'll finish up for today,' said Joel. 'It's called advocacy. As we said, if customers have a positive experience, they're more likely to come back. But if you want them to recommend your business to others, you'll have to go further.'

'I've always believed that if you give customers an outstanding experience, they'll feel compelled to tell others,' said Howard.

'Aim for that. But please don't rely on it. You need a more proactive approach.'

'But I can't exactly force customers to recommend us to other people,' said Howard.

'True. You can't *force* them. But you can give your customers a gentle nudge by respectfully asking them to refer relevant prospects to you. Encouraging satisfied customers to become your advocates is particularly effective because it draws on the power of trust that we discussed earlier. But this time, it's one step removed from you: it's the power of the relationships between your customers and *their* networks. A potential customer is much more likely to listen to their friend's recommendation than a supplier's marketing campaign. There's a pre-existing level of trust there, and no self-serving agenda.'

'Everyone knows about the importance of word of mouth,' said Howard. 'But I've never tried to seek it proactively. It either happens or it doesn't. How do you prompt it?'

'One powerful way is via a customer referral program. It can be as simple as sending an email to your best customers and politely asking if they could forward it to their network in exchange for something of value to them – like discounts or a gift of some kind. You could apply the same strategy for customers who "like" your business on Facebook, or create competitions to encourage tweeting, liking or other viral activity. You could encourage bloggers to write about your products and services. The possibilities are endless. How do you think you could encourage advocacy in your business?'

'I guess if we start running content marketing events for law firms and foreign banks, we could just ask invitees to bring along colleagues from other firms. We could offer a gift or a raffle or something.'

'Good idea. Write it down. And keep thinking of other examples. Remember, this is where the business-building process loops back in a never-ending cycle. If you can encourage your customers to become your advocates, they'll create awareness for you, thereby bringing more people into the cycle, which will in turn generate more advocates, and so on – ultimately building a self-perpetuating, ever-growing customer base.'

—

A few days after his meeting with Joel, Howard reviewed the marketing strategies with his team and selected a few to implement immediately. Within six months, they'd created a significant piece of content marketing in the form of a ten-year commemorative compliance report containing insights from experts in the field, including top-tier law firms. They'd also held an informative, content-rich workshop for foreign banks in the UK, focusing on best practice compliance management strategies.

Based on Joel's advice around upselling and cross-selling, VinciWorks aggregated all its individual e-learning courses into what Howard called *The Online Compliance Suite* and offered it as an upgrade to all clients. The response was overwhelming. Clients recognised the enhanced value and the vast majority were happy to upgrade and pay the higher fee. This not only increased revenue but also helped to cement relationships.

Howard's software team then added a number of new features to the Learning Management System (LMS). Chief among them was a feature called 'Nagware'. Based on a date, event or non-event, Nagware would literally nag users to fulfil tasks, such as completing their compliance training. Howard rebranded the feature-rich version of the system as *LMS Professional* and, within a very short period of time, almost 40 per cent of existing clients had upgraded and increased their average spend by 20 to 30 per cent.

However, the most successful strategy was the simplest: asking existing clients to make referrals. It resulted in one of Howard's largest law firm clients referring him to a global accounting firm. The accounting firm was keen to implement Enterprise Risk Management across their 100-plus member firms around the world. It had the potential to bring in a huge number of new recurring licence fees.

'We're making real progress!' said Howard in his next meeting with Joel. 'In fact, I just received two promising calls this morning: one from a top-ten global bank who'd like to see our anti-money laundering training, and another from a top-ten Australian law firm about reselling our risk-management products to their investment fund clients. It's a great starting point to the strategic expansion we've been talking about.'

'That's terrific,' said Joel. 'Well done.'

'Thanks. What we've implemented is really starting to work. For the first time in a while, we're truly growing and I can actually travel back to Melbourne with real-time insights into what's going on. It's a beautiful feeling.'

SUMMARY

MARKETING FOR GROWTH

To generate growth and achieve your vision, you need to think strategically about how to attract customers, satisfy them and inspire them to come back.

The speed of your growth will depend on your ability to move prospects efficiently and effectively through the following six-step (partly unconscious) decision-making process:

1. **Awareness:** Do I know you?

Nothing happens until someone becomes aware of you and your product or service.

Ask: What 'channels' would most effectively reach *your* target market?

2. **Desire:** Do I have a need for you?

People only make buying decisions when they desire something enough – which means that it must fulfil a real need or solve a real problem in their lives.

Ask: What marketing messages will you put into each channel to trigger customers' needs?

Ask: What *types* of marketing communications will you need to get your message across in each channel (e.g. online ads, websites, email offers, flyers, etc.)?

3. **Evaluation:** Do I trust you?

For expensive, risky or complicated purchases, most people need to engage in an evaluation process to determine its value and whether they trust your claims.

To build trust, use 'content marketing' by creating and distributing relevant, useful and engaging content to your target market for free ... *before they buy* (e.g. blog articles, white papers, publications, videos, ebooks, free demonstrations, free consultations, webinars, group presentations and try-before-you-buy offers).

Ask: What content could you create and deliver to build trust before purchase?

4. **Commitment:** Do I buy now?

Inspiring commitment is about converting prospects into paying customers.

How? Create urgency and reduce risk via limited-time offers, money-back guarantees, entry-level and limited-supply offers.

Ask: How will you create urgency and lower risk to inspire commitment?

5. **Return:** Do I come back?

Since it's much cheaper to keep and grow an existing customer than to acquire a new one, ask:

What will you do to ensure you're satisfying existing customers?

What will you do to grow your customer relationships – via upselling or cross-selling other products or services?

6. **Advocacy:** Do I tell others?

Encouraging satisfied customers to become advocates is effective because it draws on the pre-existing level of trust between your customers and *their* network.

While you can't *force* customers to become your advocates, you can respectfully ask them to refer prospects to you via a proactive customer referral program.

Ask: How will you proactively encourage advocacy among your satisfied customers?

FREE RESOURCES: To download concise summaries, templates and resources to help you apply the principles in this chapter, go to www.mindfulentrepreneur.co/resources

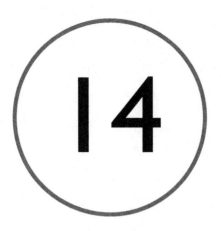

ORDEALS

Spurred on by his early success, Howard eagerly began to implement other elements of his marketing plan. And that's precisely when things began to unravel.

Having identified professional industry bodies like the Law Society and the Association of Chartered Accountants as promising channels through which to promote his products, he started approaching them. The Law Society refused. Howard soon learned that they had taken a shareholding in another risk-management company that had a kit for smaller law firms. Howard could only assume that they would eventually target the larger firms that formed VinciWorks' core client base. Not only was the Law Society no longer a viable channel, they were now a potential competitor.

Around the same time, the Solicitors Regulatory Association (SRA) decided to end the annual regulatory requirement for all lawyers to complete 16 hours of continuing professional development (CPD). In the past, they had to complete CPD to renew their legal practising certificates. Now, there would be no minimum CPD requirement and no need to complete accredited training. CPD was the bedrock of VinciWorks' training business. The goalposts were moving – and it was all seemingly beyond Howard's control.

Then, as if to rub salt into his wounds, another smaller competitor in the online learning space started to gain traction. Almost overnight, they made inroads into Howard's larger law firm market, poaching two important clients.

It all seemed like a cruel joke when one of VinciWorks' core 14 law firm clients decided to cancel their subscriptions. And almost in the same week a new compliance start-up entered the market with compliance training courses stolen directly from VinciWorks.

While this was happening, Howard received a large tax bill that he hadn't planned for. He flew back to Melbourne feeling stressed and somewhat afraid of the future. The reorganisation and systematisation, financial visibility and growth strategy should have been enough, but Howard felt under threat. Start-ups and serious competition, the end of CPD – it all seemed too much.

INTEGRATION

Howard called Aryeh for counsel. After a few minutes chit-chat, Aryeh sensed that there was a specific reason for Howard's call. He paused, giving Howard space to share his thoughts.

'Aryeh, I'm afraid. With Joel's help, we have stability and good plans and strategies in place, but it's all under threat from events and circumstances that seem totally beyond my control.'

'You've put in a lot of hard work, Howard. I can see how this would be incredibly disappointing.'

'I just wonder if there was something I could have done ...'

'You can't hope to control external events. All you can really control is how you interpret and respond to those events. That's what mindful living is all about, remember?'

'I can see things in perspective when I'm talking to you. But I just can't think that way in the moment when the tax office and my competitors and the Law Society and my clients all hit me at once.'

'You're right. New ways of thinking take time to integrate before they become second nature. It's the same for any new habit.'

'So does that mean I'll have to continue bothering you every time a problem arises?'

'It's always valuable to have someone objective to confide in and bounce ideas off. There's no substitute for a good mentor or coach. But there *are* ways to integrate the ideas we've discussed so you're less likely to be knocked off balance in the first place and find it easier to regain your composure when it happens.'

'I'm listening ...'

'Whenever you want to change a behaviour or integrate a new habit, it's not enough to simply learn how to do it once.'

'Of course not. You need to practise it. That's obvious.'

'Right. But the problem is that many people find it hard to motivate themselves to actually do the practice necessary to make it second nature. For example, before we set goals for your physical health and wellbeing, had you ever made a resolution to get fit and eat healthy?'

'Sure. Many times.'

'Well, that proves my point: if you'd kept the resolution the first time, you wouldn't have to continually remake it many times.'

'I guess I just wasn't motivated enough,' said Howard. 'And I've had other things on my mind, as you know.'

'I'm sure there are many legitimate reasons why you haven't stuck to your commitments. We all have reasons. I had an issue about writing my regular email newsletter. I struggled to find the time and perhaps motivation to sit down and write every month. Want to know how I addressed it?'

'Sure.'

'It's surprisingly simple. I designed an easy-to-follow, step-by-step writing system for me to implement each week. It included writing sessions on certain days of the week, at pre-determined times, following a specific regime. All I had to do was stick to it.'

'I know all about systems. That's Joel's mantra.'

'Has it been working?' asked Aryeh.

'Yes, actually, incredibly well. In fact, now that you mention it, I turned the commitment I made with you to lose weight and get fit into a kind of system. I run on Monday, Wednesday and Friday mornings. I also started going to a martial arts class on Tuesdays, but my travel schedule made it too difficult to keep up. So instead I've started playing golf once a week when I'm home. It's not exactly intense exercise, but I get to spend some quality time with friends, walk for four hours and hopefully improve my dreadful handicap. To be honest, I feel much healthier, more centred and more focused as a result.'

'Well, it seems I don't have to convince you, then.'

'But Joel taught me that there needs to be some accountability mechanism – some way to track that the system is performing optimally. How do you ensure you stick to it?'

'Good question. Simply having a step-by-step system is helpful – and I was able to follow it for a while. But I began to slip. So I asked a friend to call me each week, track my progress and hold me accountable. It was that simple. After three months, I didn't need the weekly calls and we dropped back to monthly.'

'That makes sense. After the first few weeks of muscle soreness, I haven't had a problem following my fitness regime. I actually enjoy it now. It's even rubbed off on Sophie and Zoe, and we sometimes run together. But if it wasn't for Andrea controlling my diet at home and constantly reminding me, while I'm away, about my commitment to cut down on carbs, I think I would've dropped it after a couple of weeks.'

'Yes, that's exactly why having a system – and a way to keep it on track – is so important. I'm glad that you've already seen it work in practice. Now you'll just need a system for maintaining your focus and balance.'

'What kind of system would I create for that?' asked Howard.

'I call it a *mindful living system*. And you should be practising it every day, at a certain time, in a certain way, just like a fitness regime. It has to become part of your life.'

'Do you do it?'

'Absolutely. For me to stay motivated, focused and balanced despite the various challenges in my life, I wake up early – usually at 6.00 a.m. while everyone else is still asleep – and I spend ten to 15 minutes completing the four key practices. It's a bit a like a meditation, but with a specific focus.'

'What four key practices are you talking about?'

'Oh, sorry,' said Aryeh with a laugh. 'They're the practices I've been teaching you. First is *purpose*. I start by recalling my core purpose. I find it powerful to remind myself that I'm working towards something worthwhile and meaningful. I then review the goals and actions I've set for each area of my life. That keeps me focused on what I need to do each day to *apply* my purpose, so it stays front and centre in my mind. That's the *application* practice.

'Sometimes all I need are those two steps. But when challenges arise that threaten to knock me off balance, I work through the *interpretation* process. I try to understand my story, test it, consider what I can learn from it, and think about the opportunities that I might not have recognised yet. It usually helps me to regain my equilibrium.

'Finally, where it's not obvious what I should be learning from my experiences, I try to engage in honest *reflection*. It requires real introspection, but it helps me to improve and ultimately moves me closer to my goals.'

'You do all that each morning – before breakfast?'

'I do. In fact, I do it three times a day. Morning, afternoon and evening. Unless there's a major issue going on in my life, it doesn't take more than ten minutes. What it does, though, is embed the practices into my consciousness. Which makes it much easier to respond calmly and mindfully when issues arise.'

'There is no way I could manage to do it three times a day,' said Howard.

'That's fine. Don't take on too much at once. Start small. Once a day for five to ten minutes is enough. You can build from there.'

'I suppose I could incorporate it into my morning run. That gives me some time to think without too many distractions. But isn't it a bit like the fitness regime – you start strong and then drop off after a few weeks? How do *you* ensure you stay on track and accountable?'

'The same as with my email newsletter,' said Aryeh. 'I have my own mentor. And I meet him regularly.'

So even a mentor needs a mentor, thought Howard, as he wondered what kind of person would be able to mentor Aryeh. Just then a text message beeped on his phone, breaking his train of thought.

It was a reminder to sort out his immediate tax problem. Howard's anxiety surged again.

'Is this system really going to help me deal with actual problems like my current tax bill?' he asked.

'It won't give you a magical tax payment solution on the spot, if that's what you're after,' said Aryeh. 'But it will help you retain your balance and composure so you can more rationally think through what the best solution might be and how to avoid that kind of situation in the future. Why don't we test it out now?'

Howard worked through the four practices with Aryeh's guidance. In the process, the 'story' that the end of CPD spelled the demise of his business began to unravel. VinciWorks was positioned as a provider of compliance training. CPD accreditation was just a secondary benefit. The legislative and regulatory requirements for mandatory compliance training were still in force. Firms would still have to demonstrate that they provide ongoing compliance training for topics such as anti-money laundering, counter terrorism and anti-bribery. Howard realised that the cancellation of CPD in the UK was probably a much bigger problem for some of his competitors than it was for VinciWorks.

VinciWorks also focused on global firms. Cancellation of UK CPD was only an issue in one of the many jurisdictions in which they needed to show compliance. Surprising himself with his ability to reframe a threatening event as an opportunity, Howard even thought about using the event to reposition the company and further distinguish it in the market. It was hard to discipline himself to work through the steps – his mind wandered regularly – and he hadn't yet come up with solutions to all his issues, but he felt more empowered to find them.

'I'll admit the practices are helpful,' Howard said. 'I just don't think I'll have the discipline to do it *every* day.'

'Well, you said that you'd try to incorporate it into your morning runs. And you run three times a week, right?'

'Yeah, I see what you're saying. I suppose three times a week is manageable. But you still haven't told me how I'm going to stay accountable?'

'Would you like to set up a regular time for us to meet – perhaps once a month? I could help to keep you on track.'

'Only if you go easy on me,' said Howard.

'Oh, you're not going to know what hit you!'

SUMMARY

INTEGRATION

You can't control external events in your life.

But regularly working through the four key mindfulness practices — **purpose, application, interpretation and reflection** — increases your resilience when challenges occur.

New ways of thinking take time to integrate before becoming second nature — like any new habit.

Make the four practices part of your life by integrating them as a step-by-step system that you practise every day, at a specific time, in a specific way — even for just five to ten minutes.

Here's how:

» Remind yourself of your core **purpose**, and check if you're still acting in alignment, so you know you're working towards something meaningful and fulfilling.

- Ask yourself: are you still aligned to your purpose?

» Review the goals and actions you've set for each area of your life to keep you focused on what you need to do each day to **apply** your purpose.

- Ask yourself: are you still on track to achieve your goals?

» When challenges arise and threaten to knock you off balance, work through the **interpretation** process.

- Ask yourself: (i) What story am I telling? (ii) What evidence might support a different interpretation? (iii) What can I learn from the experience? and (iv) What opportunities might arise?

» Where it's not obvious what you should be learning from your experiences, engage in honest **reflection** to help you improve and move closer to your goals.

- Ask yourself: why didn't I achieve my objective and what can I learn about myself from this experience?

As with any system, ensure you have an accountability mechanism in place – like a good mentor or coach – to keep you on track.

FREE RESOURCES: To download concise summaries, templates and resources to help you apply the principles in this chapter, go to www.mindfulentrepreneur.co/resources

THE ROAD BACK

Howard began monthly Skype meetings with Aryeh. Before long, he was also spending ten minutes on three mornings a week – usually during his morning runs – working through the four mindfulness practices he'd learned. He knew it wasn't a coincidence that he was also feeling better able to cope with the challenges he'd been facing.

But the transition wasn't just internal. VinciWorks' staff began to notice, too. One afternoon, Howard overheard Dean, who had been with the company during the cash-flow crisis, telling newer staff about how lucky they were.

'We used to be terrified whenever Howard came back to London,' said Dean. 'He was usually short-tempered, impatient and stressed-out. We used to call him "Hurricane Howard". When he'd arrive, the safest strategy was to batten down the hatches and hope to avoid any direct contact. Now, he's like a different person.'

Things at home were also improving. The regular coaching had inspired Howard to set a fixed time each week to connect with his daughters. It didn't matter whether he was at home, in Hong Kong or in London, they would do their best to spend time together.

In one of their conversations, Sophie, Howard's oldest daughter, shared the stress she felt in the lead up to her university exams. Howard listened and explained how adopting a 'learning and growth' mindset might help her cope with what comes her way, even if the result doesn't go as planned.

'Are you feeling okay, Dad?' she asked. 'Isn't it a little ironic that *you're* the one teaching me how to stay calm?'

Howard laughed. He felt proud and empowered to be the one giving wise counsel, rather than just receiving it.

It was now almost the end of the year. Howard met with Joel to review his progress and to begin planning for the coming 12 months.

'Let's start with what went well this past year,' said Joel.

'For starters, it looks like we're going to deliver 33 per cent revenue growth!' said Howard proudly, still marvelling not only at the achievement itself but at the fact that he had such information at his fingertips. 'And we're also 10 per cent above our already ambitious profit target for the year.'

'That's a really impressive result, Howard, especially considering it wasn't so long ago that you were teetering on the edge of bankruptcy. I'm happy for you.'

'Thanks, Joel. The odds of me achieving my goals skyrocketed once you helped me begin to think and plan deliberately and strategically – and to take more ownership for the business – rather than expecting things to simply fall into place.'

Howard updated Joel on some of VinciWorks' other achievements. His team was working together better than ever before. They'd reinforced VinciWorks' position as a leading provider of compliance training rather than merely CPD training, and created a new piece of software to help law firms track the new Continuing Competency Framework that had replaced the old CPD scheme.

Howard was especially proud of the content marketing strategies they'd implemented. Rather than merely delivering a sales pitch to the top members of the global accounting firm they'd been courting, his team had set up and facilitated a two-day, content-rich, risk-management workshop. The entire VinciWorks team had worked together to prepare the workshop, with animated videos, engaging exercises and facilitations, real-time online voting and branded posters. They even gave away portable mobile phone chargers to each participant, with the slogan 'VinciWorks: empowering risk management' emblazoned across them.

The workshop was well received. Shortly after, VinciWorks signed a global master services agreement, making them the exclusive provider of risk-management services and systems to the global network of member firms. Within a few months, this resulted in over £100,000 in consulting engagements and software licences. Howard forecasted that within three years, this single contract could generate a million pounds in annual recurring revenues.

Wins continued to follow in swift succession. The large Australian law firm with which Howard had been talking began to successfully sub-license versions of VinciWorks' risk-management system to their clients and were forecasting a minimum of ten sales a year. This was followed by a call from the head of advisory at another global accounting firm, requesting a similar arrangement.

'If we can keep the momentum going,' said Howard, 'we'll be well on our way to building a self-perpetuating, highly scalable business. The target is to get 100 larger law or accounting firms to resell VinciWorks' products. This alone would enable us to reach our five-year goal of £10 million in annual revenue.'

'Speaking of momentum,' said Joel, 'how do you intend to take things to the next level in the coming year?'

'Cash flow is healthy and we're ahead of budget. I feel more in control. Aside from more of the same, what else did you have in mind?'

'You're still travelling a lot, right?'

'Over 200 days last year.'

'Don't you want to reduce your travel time? Wasn't that one of your personal goals?'

'Actually, people sometimes ask me why I can't just sit on the beach and run everything from my laptop, especially given that it's a cloud-based software business.'

'What's your answer?'

'As a result of the systems we've put in place, I *could* run the operational parts of the business from anywhere in the world. Based on our organisational structure, those aren't even my tasks any more. *My* responsibility is to strategically grow the business; you taught me that. I wasn't doing it before, which is one of the reasons we didn't grow.

'But I've learned that strategically growing a business – virtually – is a myth. I can do a lot from home, but I need to meet people and explore opportunities. I feel like there are thousands of potential opportunities out there and unless I put myself in their path, physically, I won't catch them.'

'I can see that you've really taken on this idea of being the entrepreneur in your business rather than merely the technician, which is great. But wasn't one of your core values to be with your family? Didn't you want to spend more than 75 per cent of your time with them?'

Howard lowered his head. He had been avoiding this issue, and Joel's question had pierced the armoured exterior of his 'road warrior' persona. He *had* made significant changes, based on the commitments he made with Aryeh. He was staying for at least two weeks each time he came home, and he was rarely away for more than six weeks at a time. But, as things stood, he was still away for over 200 days – or more than 60 per cent of the year. It was well below his target of being home for 75 per cent of the year.

'You're right,' Howard said. 'I'm not in alignment right now. But what choice do I have? The business is growing, there's money in the bank and things are running smoothly, even when I'm not there. But it's not yet ready to run entirely without me, nor is it ready to sell for a worthwhile amount. And, even if I could find a CEO to replace me, I don't think I'd want to. I'm really enjoying the role, and it'd be too risky to bring in someone new when we've made such good progress and built momentum. What would you suggest I do?'

'I'm not sure. It sounds more like a personal, lifestyle decision than a business one. Why don't you speak with Andrea?'

'That's a good idea.'

Howard and Joel continued to work on the last components of the strategic plan, but Howard wasn't entirely present. Joel's question continued to churn in his mind. *Wasn't one of your core values to be with your family?* The question had brought the misalignment between his core values and his current actions into sharp focus. He was home for another week, and he knew he had to deal with the issue before he left for London again.

At home that evening, Howard was preoccupied and pensive. Andrea noticed immediately.

'Did something happen at work today?' she asked. 'You look worried.'

'Nothing special. I'm just feeling out of alignment.'

'What?'

'You know, not being home enough. Not spending enough time with you and the kids.'

'We agreed that you'd have to travel for a while, just until the business gets back on track and things calm down.'

'I know. And things *have* calmed down. In many ways, I feel like a different person. When things were tight, I didn't want to worry you by sharing how I felt when the bank would call each month demanding payment of our overdrawn accounts. Honestly, I wanted to crawl into a hole and never come out. I'm so thankful that I no longer have to deal with those calls.'

'You didn't have to tell me, Howard. I could see it on your face. And I can also see the difference now.'

'Yeah, well, it's not enough. I've tried to tell myself that being away so often is okay and that it's just for a little while. But it's not okay. The girls feel it. I know you feel it. I just don't see what other options I have.' Howard's phone beeped. He looked down to see a text message from Josh requesting a Skype call. 'And, as you can see, even when I'm physically at home, I still can't stop work from intruding. I realise that I wouldn't have a business in the first place if it wasn't for digital technology, but sometimes it's suffocating.'

'We've made it through tougher challenges and we'll get through this one, too.'

Howard appreciated her strength and optimism. As usual, he knew she was right.

'You said Aryeh taught you all those practices for balance and alignment,' Andrea said. 'Aren't they helping?'

'I've been trying to work through them regularly. And they've generally been very helpful. But when Joel confronted me today about the issue of being away from home, I realised that I've been avoiding it – probably because I feel so guilty.'

'Don't beat yourself up. And cut the victim crap – that's not you, and it's not us. Let's work through Aryeh's process together.'

'Okay. I'm supposed to reflect on my core purpose, and whether I'm in alignment. Right now, I don't feel very aligned. Being a good husband and father are core values for me and yet more often than not I'm thousands of miles away. I know we make an effort to talk on Skype and text each other, but it's not the same.'

Andrea was silent. Howard could see that she shared his views. 'So what are you supposed to do next, to realign yourself?' she eventually asked.

'I'm supposed to set goals and action plans for living my values in each area of my life, and then review my progress each day to ensure I'm on track. It's about living more intentionally. I did this almost 90 days ago with Aryeh, so it's time for me to set new goals and action plans for the coming 90 days.'

'What goals did you set last time?'

'I said that I wanted to communicate with you and the kids more regularly. I wanted to be more in tune with what was happening in your lives.'

'I think you've done that. We do talk more often. The kids have noticed that you now make time for them.'

'But I've taken seven return flights to London from Melbourne and travelled over 137,000 miles in the last five months! One stewardess recognised me from a previous flight. We began talking and I realised that I actually fly more miles than she does!'

'Yes, but you've been away for shorter periods and you're coming home more often. That's a good thing.'

'I know, but it's not enough – in quantity or in quality. I'm always on call. I just can't switch off and concentrate on enjoying our time together. Digital technology underpins the business and it's enabled us to communicate while I'm away, but it's also detracting from our personal, direct, human communication when I'm home. If I wanted to be totally single-minded, I could continue doing this. But in the long term, it'll damage my relationship with you and the kids, not to mention my sense of wellbeing.'

'Okay, so what can we do?'

'I need to set new goals for the family area of my life. People laugh when I tell them your joke that business travel is the answer to a happy marriage, but it's only true in moderation. Isn't it?'

'Yes, of course. I think there's something positive about you going away every now and then. But there's a limit.'

'I'm glad you said that,' said Howard, relieved that Andrea wanted him home more often. 'We need to find a way for us to be together, as a family, at least 70 to 80 per cent of the time.'

'I'd really like that – as long as you remember to turn the lights off when you leave a room, put down the toilet seat and take out the rubbish bins on Tuesday nights.'

Howard laughed. 'I'll try. But the challenge is how to actually make it happen. I can't leave the business to run itself yet, putting another CEO in place right now is risky, and it's not yet time to sell.'

'This might seem radical,' suggested Andrea, 'but what if we all moved back to London together, as a family? We'd obviously have to wait until Zoe finishes her final year of high school, so it couldn't be for at least another nine months. But after that, why not?'

Howard considered the idea. They were both originally from London, and many of their close family members were still living there. 'We'd have to run it by the kids, but I'd be open to moving if you are. The bulk of our clients are there, our family is there. It actually makes a lot of sense.'

Howard and Andrea mapped out a 90-day action plan to explore whether moving to London could work and how to make it happen.

'I like this process,' Andrea said.

'We're not finished just yet. Whether or not we move, I'd also like to set a goal around more quality time together and more time to just switch off and recharge – without all those digital distractions.'

Almost on cue, Howard's watch and phone buzzed and beeped simultaneously. They both laughed.

'Well, what exactly do you have in mind?' asked Andrea.

'I'm not quite sure, but Aryeh once described his weekly ritual of spending an entire 24-hour period without technology. He switches off his phone, computer and TV and focuses on connecting with his wife, kids, close friends and himself. For him, it also has religious significance – it's his Sabbath – but maybe we could adopt a scaled-down version of that?'

'Like a digital Sabbath?'

'Yeah, I like that term.' *Digital Sabbath*, Howard repeated to himself. 'Do you think the kids would be into it?'

'I suppose we could start with a Friday night dinner at home together as a family, no phones, computers or TV, and then build from there. I think they could handle that. Leave that one with me; I'll talk to them and make it happen.'

Howard smiled. He already felt better.

'Are there any more steps to work through?' Andrea asked.

'There are two more. But one is for when I experience specific challenges that threaten to knock me off balance. It's about being more intentional around how I interpret events, rather than simply responding reactively. It's easy to tell a doom-and-gloom story about challenging experiences, but I've found that with some gentle reality-testing, it loses some of its negative impact. In fact, those seemingly negative events can actually lead to growth and new opportunities.'

'I've noticed that you've generally seemed calmer and less stressed over the last few months, but I didn't realise that this is what you've been doing.'

Howard laughed. 'I try to do it at least three times a week, during my morning run. It really helps. I'm glad you've noticed.'

'Take the conversation we're having right now. Even six months ago, we wouldn't have been able to work through these issues without one of us getting upset. The girls and I would often feel like we were treading on eggshells around you. One wrong step and you'd either fly off the handle or shut down completely.'

'Was I really that bad?'

'We knew you were under pressure. We knew you weren't sleeping well. You weren't running or playing golf or doing anything other than working and fighting for survival. For *our* survival. We knew that, so we just tried to avoid being the cause of further stress.'

Howard shared Dean's conversation with the new VinciWorks staff about 'Hurricane Howard'. Andrea laughed out loud.

'You know, listening to you now, I realise how grateful I should be to both Joel and Aryeh,' said Howard. 'I can't even relate to Hurricane Howard any more. I hope none of you ever need to meet him again. But it's a good example of how what seemed like such a negative situation at the time can lead to learning and growth.'

'So does this mean that the next time I get angry at you for leaving the toilet seat up, you'll see it as an opportunity to grow and learn?' Andrea asked him.

Howard rolled his eyes and feigned a disapproving look.

'Okay, Mr Cool, Calm and Collected, what's the last step in the process?'

'I'll tell you, as long as you don't use it against me. Where it's not obvious what I should be learning from my experiences, the idea is to engage in honest self-reflection. That's what helped me finally realise that although I've always been the owner *of* my business, I wasn't taking ownership *for* the business. It was a draining process, but it definitely helped me move closer to my goals.'

'Maybe I should be adopting these practices, too,' said Andrea.

'I agree. And so should the kids. We could even discuss it as a family on Friday night.'

'Creating a distraction-free zone will be hard enough. Let's just get them to the table first. Then we can worry about introducing them to new practices.'

That night Howard resisted the urge to check his emails. He turned off his phone and, instead of putting his laptop into standby mode, he shut it down completely. He hugged Andrea and rolled over with a real sense of satisfaction, knowing that today he'd moved another step closer to living in alignment with his purpose.

EXIT STRATEGY

Howard felt exhilarated. He was back in London and had just emerged from a meeting with the managing partner of one of the fastest-growing and most innovative law firms in the UK. The firm had managed to entirely systematise their activities to the point where they could confidently outsource their back office – and much of the procedural aspects of their legal work – to lower-cost people in a lower-cost location. And, critically, they achieved this without diminishing the quality of their services. In fact, their back-office systems were now so proficient that they had begun offering the service to *other* law firms, creating a new revenue stream for them while helping their law firm clients to reduce their costs and increase profitability.

But it wasn't just their business model that excited Howard. The managing partner had laid out plans to float the company for a nine-figure sum – which Howard quickly worked out to be in excess of £100 million – and he asked Howard if VinciWorks would be interested in partnering with them and going public on the UK stock exchange. As a Software-as-a-Service technology business focused on the governance risk and compliance sector, with over 30 per cent annual growth and over 60 per cent of the world's largest law firms as clients, the managing partner felt that VinciWorks might just add the critical 'sizzle' to their Initial Public Offering (IPO).

Howard immediately called Joel to discuss the opportunity.

'Nothing's set in stone, and it might just be a pipe dream, but if we could get 10 per cent of the £100 million sale price, I could exit the business with £10 million within the next three years. That's exactly my stretch goal.'

'That's really exciting,' said Joel. 'And whether or not this specific opportunity materialises for you, the fact that you're having these kinds of conversations says a lot about how far you've come. Out of interest, though, what would you do with yourself if you did leave the business?'

'You mean aside from taking a long holiday with Andrea and the kids, sitting on a beach sipping cocktails all day?'

'Remember, Howard, I know you. You couldn't sit still for very long – even with a cocktail. Your "greatest sustainable value" purpose would gnaw at you every day.'

'It's funny you say that. I've actually been thinking about it. But, before I answer, I have a question for you: what's happening with your goal of scaling *your* business?'

'I'm still keen to do it but I haven't pushed it forward yet, if that's what you're asking.'

'It seems we've come full circle then. Remember when you first came to my office, you asked me to help you leverage your business online?'

'Yes, I do. We never got around to discussing it, though.'

'Having personally experienced your process, I have a few ideas for how to leverage business coaching in the online space. In fact, I'd love to partner with you in building an online business that offers high-quality, affordable business coaching and training services to small- and medium-size enterprises.

'Together we've proven that your business strategies and processes work. And VinciWorks has the experience and resources to turn them into engaging online training. We could support the content with templates, workbooks, digital marketing services and online coaching.'

'Seriously? That would be great. I'd love to do it together. It would also tie in perfectly with the book.'

'What book?' asked Howard, confused.

'I haven't mentioned this to you yet, but I've been writing a book about your experiences. I think your journey from near bankruptcy and emotional distress to business success and personal fulfilment would help a lot of people. And not just the business strategy side, but Aryeh's intentional and mindful living practices, too. I see it as a holistic manual for surviving and thriving in business and in life.'

'Joel, I don't know if I'm comfortable with you sharing my personal experiences …' Howard's voice trailed off as he recalled the 3.00 a.m. wake-ups, the overdue bills and his general sense of hopelessness. 'Actually, let me take that back. If the book can free others from being slaves to their businesses like I was, it'll be worthwhile. In fact, if you're interested, I'd even be happy to help you with the book as well.'

'That's great; and we'll need to rope in Aryeh, too.'

'We need to write a business plan,' said Howard. 'Shall I teach you how to write one? I can introduce you to a great coach!'

'I'll call you if I need help,' said Joel with a smile, as he wondered where this new opportunity might take them on their respective journeys.

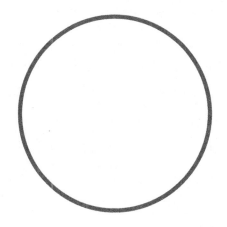

CONCLUSION

Whether or not your situation is as bleak as Howard's once was, if you've read this book, chances are you're also facing some challenges. Perhaps your business isn't giving you the income you need to fund the lifestyle you desire. Perhaps it feels like it's all your responsibility, consuming your time and energy and not leaving space for other areas of your life. Or perhaps it's creating stress that's affecting your sense of balance, motivation and fulfilment.

While you can't eliminate the obstacles that will inevitably arise, Howard's story demonstrates that there are practical steps you can take to spark rapid growth, free yourself from the day-to-day grind and enhance your sense of fulfilment. And even though Howard's situation is unique, the core principles that he applied are relevant to almost every small- to medium-sized business.

What are those core principles? The foundation of business building is the recognition that it's simply not enough to be skilled at the *technical aspects* of your work. If you want to be successful, you also need to become a skilled *entrepreneur*. This means you need to begin working *on* your business, not just *in* it. What does working *on* your business mean for you, practically? It depends on your goals.

If your goal is to achieve more time, space and freedom, it's important to design your business to run smoothly and predictably – with or without you. To do that, you'll need to create four kinds of 'clarity': (1) structural clarity, so you know *what* jobs need to happen and *who's* responsible for them; (2) job clarity, so you know exactly what's expected in each of those jobs; (3) task clarity, so you know *how* to perform the key tasks within each job – ideally via step-by-step systems, much like franchises have; and (4) performance clarity, so you and your team know how you're performing and whether you're achieving the intended results. With that kind of clarity, you'll be well on your way to creating a 'turn-key operation' that can effectively run without you.

If your goal is to achieve rapid growth – including more customers, revenue and profit – you'll also need to define your overall business strategy, just like Howard did when he created his strategic plan. For example, which markets should you target? How will you differentiate your business in those markets? How will you measure your growth? These strategic questions are the essential foundation for executing your growth strategy.

However, the speed of your growth will depend on your ability to move prospective customers through the six-step journey they undertake when making purchase decisions: from Awareness, Desire and Evaluation through to Commitment, Return and Advocacy. Developing your marketing system around these steps is crucial to building a self-perpetuating, ever-growing customer base.

Finally, as we have seen, the state of one's business and one's state of mind are deeply interconnected. Which is why you'll need to take a holistic approach to achieve the dual outcomes you're really after: a successful business *and* a true sense of internal ful-filment. That means engaging in four key mindfulness practices: (1) defining what's important to you – your core values – via a clear, inspiring *purpose* statement; (2) creating a plan for *applying* those values in each area of your life; (3) drawing on your ability to *interpret* challenges and disappointments realistically and through a growth- and opportunity-oriented lens; and (4) engaging in a process of *self-reflection* to derive lessons for change when the insights aren't obvious. In order to stay sane, focused and motivated when faced with challenges, you'll need to *integrate* these insights into your life via a system that you apply regularly – it's not enough to do it reactively.

Ultimately, you cannot control the external events that will impact your business and your life. But what you can do is to start taking more responsibility – more ownership – for the way you plan for and respond to those events. You can become more strategic, more deliberate and more intentional about the way you run your business and the way you run your life. When you do this, you'll begin to shape your own reality to a greater extent than you ever thought possible. And that's really what being a Mindful Entrepreneur is all about.

GET YOUR FREE RESOURCES

Gain access to a range of FREE resources, including practical summaries, tools and templates designed to help you apply the strategies contained in *The Mindful Entrepreneur* to your business and your life.

You'll receive:

- A **comprehensive summary of each key topic** in the book, with details that build on the chapter summaries;
- **User-friendly diagrams** and **step-by-step tools** for implementing the strategies in each topic; and
- **Practical, fill-in-the-blank templates** to help you apply each strategy immediately.

If you want the resources to help you apply the same proven, step-by-step system that Howard used to **spark rapid growth**, **free up his time** and **enhance his sense of fulfilment**, go to:

www.mindfulentrepreneur.co/resources

Printed in Great Britain
by Amazon

24328222R00150